Musing Christian Principles

An Old Man Thinking About Life

Martin Murphy

Musing Christian Principles

Copyright © 2018 by Martin Murphy

All rights reserved. No part of this book may be reproduced or transmitted in any form or by any means without written permission of the author.

ISBN 9781732437944

To: Nat, who understands life

Introduction

The sub-title of this book is: "An Old Man Thinking About Life." Therefore, this book is a reflection of my thoughts. It's not meek Martin writing and certainly not an intended caricature of my accomplishments, because I'm neither of those. I simply love to search for the truth.

Rational life principles are not popular in the postmodern culture. For the past 35 years I've pondered theological propositions and for the past 25 years I've mused cultural principles. The serious questions about life are still hidden in the mysterious box. Each day I try to open the box of mysteries to find answers to the preponderous questions of life. Although I spurned academic pursuits early in life, I embraced the academy for the better part of a decade in mid-life. The mystery box still waits for me. I was told not to talk to myself, so I decided to write down some thoughts to ponder and muse. For most of my 72 years each day has been a learning experience. This book is a brief summary of conversations intended to satisfy my inquiries about life.

FOREWORD

In 1517 a man named Martin nailed 95 Theses to a church door. This act is often portrayed as a kind of atypical ultimatum, as if nailing them to the door was a defiant "in-your-face" thing. Actually, it was quite common at the time to do it that way to bring up topics for debate. The items on the list were varied but related topics presented for discussion and consideration. God the Holy Spirit took something that was common and used it as the spark to ignite the blaze of Reformation, which had already been poised to break out for well over a hundred years. It was in a sense the straw that broke the camel's back.

This year, five hundred and one years later, another man named Martin presented sixty topics in a book, varied but related, and with a heart to do the same thing: reform the church and bring light to the culture. They are in a sense nailed to the figurative "door" of the church. Of course, the church is not a physical building or meeting place, but God's people, as the contemporary Martin so aptly proves in this writing.

Martin will no doubt be embarrassed by my comparison because he is an unassuming and humble man. But make no mistake, this collection of writings has as its common thread a clarion call to return to Scripture and to the principles of the Reformation and instill them into the church of our day.

I have known Martin Murphy for many years and I know him to be a man with a pastor's heart. He has an exceptional gift to guide and encourage God's people. *Musing Christian Principles* is a compendium of wisdom from a sage. It is challenging and thought-provoking. It is a buffet of the cold hard truth served up with politically incorrect saltiness, and seasoned with barbs of delicious irony. There is no lack of religious incorrectness either. Martin does not hold back in his accurate and not-so-painless assessment of the contemporary church with such statements as, "The how-to gospel has bankrupted the evangelical church." Jewels of humor jump off the pages, such as "Ecclesiastical intrigue is as common as fried chicken."

Musing Christian Principles contain wisdom collected after years of experience gathering insight into the workings and meaning of the contemporary church, the society around it, and the interaction of the two. He writes to bring the "life" of the reformation back into our life. It brings to mind Isaiah 58:12 – "Those from among you shall build the old waste places; you shall raise up the foundations of many generations; and you shall be called the Repairer of the Breach, The Restorer of Streets to Dwell In."

N. G. Rudulph, Jr.
Selma, Alabama
November 2018

Table of Contents

1. Church at the Meeting House 1
2. 85 Year Old Gave Up On Church 4
3. Demythologize the Church 6
4. Who Are the "Dones" 10
5. Invite Unbelievers to Church, Invite Believers to Worship 12
6. Is Communication Technology Good or Bad? 15
7. Ministry of the Church 17
8. Mission of the Church 20
9. No Men In Israel 23
10. Protestant Denominationalism 26
11. Purpose of the Church 28
12. Theological Integrity 30
13. Assurance of Grace and Salvation (Part 1) 33
14. Assurance of Grace and Salvation (Part 2) 36
15. Be a Friend of God 38
16. Biblical Interpretation Under Siege 40
17. Broken Promises 42
18. Who Is Independent? 47
19. Christmas (Part 1) 54
20. Christmas (Part 2) 57
21. Disappearance of Ultimate Authority 60
22. Easter 62

23. Examples of Theological Ignorance 66
24. Forgiveness 68
25. God's Covenant Promises 71
26. God's Mouthpiece 73
27. God's People are Praying People 77
28. Hell Is Real 80
29. Is the Word of God Enough? 83
30. True Gospel: Forensic Justification 85
31. Make the Church Great Again 90
32. Thanksgiving 92
33. The Soul of Man 95
34. Where Is My Eternal Home? 98
35. Worship According to God's Standard 100
36. I Apologize for My Apology 102
37. Church Growth 104
38. Religious Activity is Killing the Professing Church 107
39. Are You Being Reformed by the Word of God? 109
40. Biblical Reformation Is Not Neutral 112
41. Clarion Call to the Church 118
42. Is Your Conscience Held Captive to the Word of God? 121
43. Hope and Vision for Reformation 124
44. Judgment For the Unreformed Church 127
45. Cultural Dilemma 131
46. Egalitarianism and Racial Ignorance 133
47. Entertainment Replaces Truth 137

48. Sense, Reason, and Intellect 140
49. Image Is Not Everything 143
50. Is the Debate Table Closed? 145
51. Postmodern Culture Accommodates the Church 147
52. Terrorism Strikes Again 150
53. What Does Your World Look Like? 152
54. Sophism is Stealthy Deception 156
55. Feminism in the American Culture 159
56. Victimizationalism 162
57. Consumerism: The Worldview That Makes People Happy 164
58. Pragmatism: The Worldview That Works 166
59. Education: The Great Human Challenge 169
60. The Benediction 175

1. Church at the Meeting House

The "dones" are professing Christians who maintain a relationship with God, but have no use for what they perceive to be the "church." To put it another way, they are done with the church. What they perceive is probably not reality! Image is not everything. For nearly 15 years I have pleaded with professing Christians to quit "going to church" in the sense of going to a "place" called by the name "(such and such) church." Over the past couple of years, I've heard more and more people tell me "I quit going to church." I know what they mean, but my response is, "no, you did not quit going to church, because you are the church" if you are a Christian! You may have quit going to a place or building referred to as the "church." Maybe you are merely a professing Christian and in that case you never became part of the body of Christ (the church). The expression, "going to church" is a bad habit that has endured for at least 150 years in this country. Christians ought to recover the Puritan expression, "the church assembled at the Meeting House." Recently, I heard a conversation between a couple of people and one said to the other, "missed you in church last Sunday." I thought to myself, "He doesn't know what the church is." If he had simply said, "the church missed you last Sunday" I probably would not be writing this book. Instead of going to church, professing Christians need to do what the church is supposed to do, according to the Word of God.

The purpose of the church is to worship (privately, with the family, and collectively as a local congregation) and take pleasure in worshipping the triune God. The church has a mandate to be engaged in the mission of the church. The mission of the church is to make disciples (that is where evangelism comes in, but evangelism is not the only aspect of the mission) and to live a holy life (not perfection, in any sense of the word), both of which require a serious study of the Word of God. The ministry of the church means to serve the Lord with your individual gifts and ability according to the instruction of the elders (pastor and teachers) of the church. The church is NOT a piece of property, a building, an institution, a denomination, or a place to go; The church is the people of God.

The reason so many in this generation are "done" with the church is that they do not know what the church is. Furthermore, from my 30 plus years of experience many professing Christians do not understand the nature of the church. Why? The reason is they are not taught from the full counsel of God the nature of the church, the purpose of the church, the mission of the church, and the ministry of the church by the leadership of the church. If the pulpit does not know what the church is, how is the pew supposed to know?

The following is a brief quote from the chapter, "Holy Catholic Church" in my book, *The Essence of Christian Doctrine*.

> Given the biblical teaching on the nature of the church what does Jesus mean when He said, "I will build my church?" Does the Lord mean that He would build a building? The inspired apostle Paul says no. "And what agreement has the temple of God with idols? For you are the temple of the living God. As God has said: I will dwell in them and walk among them. I will be their God and they shall be My people" (2 Corinthians. 6:16).
>
> Many if not most professing Christians think of the church in terms of a physical piece of architecture. The place or building where professing Christians assemble for worship, Bible study, and fellowship has become a synonym for the church. I cannot begin to describe how much suffering has accompanied the terrible mistake of calling the building where Christians assemble for worship, instruction, and fellowship, a church. Is the building where the name of the church appears on a sign or a marquee the church? The place where Christians assemble for worship or Bible study is not a church. The church is a spiritual building, built by God. The church in biblical terms is not a building made by men, but rather a building created in the image of God. The Holy Spirit resides in the building called the church. "Living stones" is the description given by Peter for those who form and shape God's building (See 1 Peter 2:5). This must mean that God's building consists of the souls of Christians filled with the Holy Spirit of God.

The inspired words of the apostle Paul in his letter to Timothy says, "I write so that you may know how one ought to conduct himself in the household of God, which is the church of the living God, the pillar and support of the truth" (1 Timothy. 3:15). Truth and nothing but the truth is acceptable in God's building (the church). Falsehood and lies are not acceptable. The church is supposed to distribute truth; the truth about God, the truth about man, the truth about how to live, the truth about eternity, and all the truth from the Word of God.

If the church distributes truth, Christians must have a true understanding of the church rather than a false understanding of the church. Unfortunately the church has traditionally served as the center of social and cultural functions, thus associating the church with a building or an organization. It was the building that provided entertainment to the body rather than enrichment to the soul. Many have sadly adopted the view that a church is nothing more than a building and a membership roll.

It is difficult to set aside old habits and tradition passed on from previous generations. Even so, I hope you will reconsider the nature of the church and re-examine what the Bible has to say about the church. The nature of the church is inseparably connected with the nature of Jesus Christ. To ignore the true biblical teaching on the nature of the church is to ignore Jesus Christ. (*The Essence of Christian Doctrine*, by Martin Murphy, p. 56-57)

2. 85 Year Old Gave Up On Church

An article was posted on Facebook titled "10 Reasons You Should Go to Church Every Week." There were many replies but one was particularly eye-opening:

> I am 85 love the lord with all my heart and worked for him most of my life but i gave up on church 6 years ago and been vastly happier since it is no more gossip, more cliques no more loud wild music i cannot take and no more politics in church and no one more people playing Christian. Now i still pray daily help others read the word and listen to sermons by Dr Stanley and others on internet and do bible studies on line and feel more peaceful relaxed and good than in long long time ,wish i had done this years ago when the church started "getting modernized" to the point where i felt God and the Holy Spirit was missing mostly altogether .so much hypocrisy n the church today it is like the Church of Laodicea.

Most professing Christians do not understand the meaning of the word "church." The biblical meaning is amazingly simple: The people of God. One Christian Catechism states it this way: "The invisible church is the whole number of God's children that have been, are, or shall be gathered into one under Christ the head. The church literally refers to the children of God in every age in every place "that have been, are, or shall be gathered into one under Christ the head." Then there are local congregations of PROFESSING Christians, some of them are certainly NOT Christians and some are Christians. Local congregations must conduct worship and meetings "decently and in order" (1 Corinthians 14:40). The 85 year old woman still does not understand the nature, purpose, mission, and ministry of the church. She said, "I gave up on church" which is another impossible use of the word "church." A true Christian cannot give up on the church no more the one can give up on Jesus Christ. A person "goes to church" one time in their life; Then that person becomes an integral part of the church and will spend his or her lifetime going to worship, going to prayer meeting, going to take the ordinances prescribed by Jesus Christ, going to fellowship, et al. The church is active in its duties required by God. It is also passive because it is God that adds to the number each day. The sad truth is that the 85 year old woman was never taught the Word of God in its fullness, which is the mission of the church. God sends a warning to all leaders, teachers, and elders who have not carried out their responsibilities to disciple the church with the whole counsel of God. "My brethren, let not many of you become teachers, knowing that we shall receive a stricter judgment" (James 3:1).

I pray for reformation in the evangelical church in particular and the visible church in general.

3. Demythologize the Church

Jesus mentioned the church a few times in the New Testament, but He didn't devote a chapter to define the nature, purpose, mission, and ministry of the church. However, Jesus left the church this promise: "I will build my church" (Matthew 16:18). The word church found in the New Testament has been misused and misinterpreted throughout the history of the church. It is my purpose to share some thoughts on the nature of the church. The great challenge is to demythologize the church. This brief list will help:

> The church is not someplace you go to
> The church is not a building
> The church is not an institution
> The church is not owned by anyone on this planet
> The church is not graded by ethnicity, importance, or social status
> The church is not divided by doctrine

What is the church? Hold on to your hat because the answer is simple, but it will blow you away. The church is the people of God. Christians living in a specific geographical area gather together as the church to fulfill the purpose, mission, and ministry of the church; specifically, but not limited to: collective worship according to the Word of God, preaching, teaching, fellowship, and prayer.

The church is not singularly identified. It is embodied within two dimensions commonly known as the visible church and the invisible church.

The church visible is mixed with wheat and tares. One prominent church creed describes the visible church as the whole "number of professing Christians, with their children, associated together for divine worship and godly living, agreeable to the Scriptures and submitting to the lawful government of Christ's kingdom."

The church invisible is the church in heaven. The invisible church is the true church or to put it another way the saved church. The invisible church is infallible, indestructible, indivisible, and universal.

The Bible does not have a specific proof text to prove the nature of the church. The full counsel of God must be consulted to discover the nature of the church. The Bible does use metaphors that describe the nature of the church. A metaphor is a figure of speech that draws a comparison between two things. The comparison is not literally expressed and may be understood by implication. Although space does not permit inquiry into all the biblical metaphors a few of them will suffice.

The first metaphor I bring to your attention is the vineyard (Matthew 21:33-46; John 15:1-8). The nature of the vineyard is such that it is productive. Likewise the church is productive when it fulfills the responsibilities given to the church according to the Word of God. The preaching of the Word of God has been given to the church. When the church insures the sound preaching of the Word of God, it is productive.

The field is another metaphor that will help us understand the nature of the church. The field belongs to God; the church is the field, therefore God's people belong to Him (1 Corinthians 3:5-9).

The Bible also uses another agricultural metaphor to describe the nature of the church. That metaphor found often in the gospel of John is a flock (John 10:1-16). Raising sheep was common in all ancient Near Eastern cultures. Sheep provided food, clothing, and sacrifices for religious worship. Sheep need a shepherd to feed them and protect them. The shepherd in the local church is the pastor/elder. The sheep/shepherd metaphor was a favorite of the Lord Jesus Christ. Obviously the sheep/shepherd aspect ultimately has the invisible church in mind.

One of my favorite metaphors used to describe the nature of the church is the family of God (Luke 11:13; Romans 8:14-17; Galatians 4:5-7). The nature of the church is such that order, harmony, and unity are necessary for each local congregation. The modern notion that families function best when the various parties are disaffected, is one reason that local congregations feud, fight, and divide. If children in the family can't get along, neither can siblings in the family of God.

The Bible also describes the church as a bride (Ephesians 5:22-29). The biblical bride is supposed to be pure, and so it is with the church. The biblical bride submits to, honors, and obeys the groom. The nature of the church found in the biblical bride should show us the inseparable connection of God to his bride the church.

Given the biblical teachings on the nature of the church what does Jesus mean when he said, "I will build my church?" Does the Lord mean that he would build a physical building? Many professing Christians think of the church in terms of a physical piece of architecture. The physical structures where professing Christians meet for worship, Bible study, and fellowship have become a synonym for the church. The result is a misunderstanding of the nature of the church.

The church is God's building according to the Word of God. One verse from the Bible will make the point: "And what agreement has the temple of God with idols? For you are the temple of the living God. As God has said: I will dwell in them and walk among them. I will be their God and they shall be My people" (2 Corinthians. 6:16). The church in biblical terms is not a building made by men, but rather a building created in the image of God. Notice the rhetorical question asked by the inspired apostle: "What agreement has the temple of God with idols?" None of course! God is true! An idol is false! Only truth is acceptable in God's building. Falsehood and lies are un-acceptable.

God's building consists of the souls of Christians filled with the Holy Spirit of God. If Christians would come to grips with the nature of the church maybe the seeds of revival will germinate into beautiful plants. Many Christians do not understand the nature of the church. Several generations grew up under a subjective set of rules that did not include a proper understanding of the fundamental principles that would have taken them down a different road.

The church in the south more than any part of the country has traditionally served as the center of social and cultural functions, thus associating the church with a building. It was the building that provided entertainment to the body rather than enrichment to the soul. The church in the Bible belt has been treated like a social club, civic club, country club, men's club, and women's club.

Christians must set aside the baggage from previous generations. I know it is hard to set aside old habits, but Christians should reconsider the nature of the church and re-examine what the Bible says about the nature of the church. The church has been abused, used, and amused through the centuries. Set aside the traditional views of the church and adopt the dynamic views as you find them in the Word of God. Set your goal to demythologize the church for coming generations.

4. Who Are the "Dones?"

There is a new word being tossed about in religious discussions. The "dones" is a reference to a generation of people who are "done" with the church. The "dones" are professing Christians who claim to be "done" with the church.

Jesus said, "I will build my church." Those words were inspired by God and recorded by Matthew. I don't normally refer to the Greek text, but I'm frustrated, so here is a layman friendly lesson from the Greek text. The Greek word translated "build" is from the Greek word *oikodomeo*. It is a future, active, indicative verb, which I take to be a predictive future tense. It means the action will take place in the future. It is in the active voice, which literally means "I will be building" or to put it another way it will constantly and daily take place in the future. It is in the indicative mood, which means it is an indisputable fact. What was Jesus going to build for the rest of human existence? The church, which is one of the most misused, misinterpreted, and misrepresented words in the English Bible. The Greek word inspired by the Holy Spirit, recorded by Matthew and preserved for every generation is the noun *ekklesia*. It is a compound noun derived from the preposition *ek* that means "out of." The proper Greek noun *kaleo* is literally translated "to call." So *ekklesia* (church) is literally "the called out ones."

The church consists of those people from every corner of the earth and in every generation that has belonged, now belongs, or will belong to God, because of the finished atoning work of Jesus Christ by the power of the Holy Spirit. To put it in familial terms, the church is the family of God. So the unbeliever hears the good saving news of the gospel, is convicted and enabled by the Holy Spirit to trust Jesus Christ as their personal Lord and Savior. It is "like" going to church and will be the first and last time they will ever go to church. Then that person is one out of a collective large number of the church. So what happens to the church?

Dr. David Wells in his book, *The Courage to be Protestant*, writes, "It would be quite unrealistic to think that evangelicalism today could look exactly as it did fifty years ago, or a hundred, or five hundred. At the same time, the truth by which it is constituted never changes because God, whose truth it is, never changes. There should therefore be threads of continuity that bind real Christian believing in all ages. It is some of those threads, I believe, that are now being lost."

Of all the books I've written, *The Church: First Thirty Years*, explains the "church" based on the Book of Acts, which is an infallible normative and descriptive history of the church. I challenge every Christian to read the book and see if some of the essential threads of Christianity are "being lost" as you read this brief article. As I said in the Introduction and now repeat: "The first thirty years of the church ought to be a flagship for the last thirty years of the church." The "Dones" need a flagship to follow!

5. Invite Unbelievers to Church, Invite Believers to Worship

"I'm going to church this Sunday," says Mr. Devout Christian. Mrs. Devout Christian saw her friend in the store and said, "We'd love to have you come to church this Sunday." Sometimes Christians say, "Come visit our church." These comments about the church come from religious jargon inherited from previous generations. Everyone from Sunday School children to trained theologians use terminology about the church that is not biblically consistent.

The church on earth consists of professing Christians. They profess faith in Christ and believe the basic doctrine of Holy Scripture. However, many professing Christians fail to understand the biblical doctrine of "the church." The church is not a building, a campus, or a place. It is the people who belong to God through faith in Jesus Christ by the power of the Holy Spirit. To invite someone to church means they are invited to profess faith in Christ and believe the basic doctrine of Holy Scripture by the power of the Holy Spirit. Actually, inviting someone to church is part of the mission of the church, commonly known as evangelism.

The word "gospel" literally means, "to announce good tidings or good news." It often refers to the good news of God's saving grace. The "evangel" is the good news of the message of the redemptive work of Christ. When we add "ism" to "evangel" we adopt as a world and life view the salvation message of Jesus Christ. Therefore, evangelism is the way of life for Christians.

The evangelistic enterprise begins with a "seeker." All people "should seek the Lord in the hope that they might grope for Him and find Him…" (Acts 17:27). To "grope" for the Lord implies that one is searching for something. The unbeliever attempts to find relief from the guilt of sin. The believer has a duty to make the following announcement: "Repent, and believe the gospel" (Mark 1:15). The method of evangelism used by the early evangelical church may be described as the doctrine of seeking. It was the method used by many of the English and early American Puritans, especially by the great evangelist Jonathan Edwards.

Jonathan Edwards left the church with a legacy that has almost been forgotten. The legacy was a biblical view of evangelism, a God-centered evangelism known as seeking. Unfortunately, many evangelistic messages are man-centered and that discourages the seeking doctrine. Man-centered evangelism believes that an unconverted sinner can cause God to change the sinner's heart. Its message is the unbiblical message that God certainly helps in the process of salvation, but ultimately man must save himself. Jonathan Edwards took the view that God could cause the heart to be changed and then the converted sinner could believe. Jonathan Edwards on his remarks *Concerning Efficacious Grace wrote*, "It is manifest that the Scripture supposes, that if ever men are turned from sin, God must undertake it, and he must be the doer of it; that it is his doing that must determine the matter..." (*Works of Jonathan Edwards*, Hickman ed., Volume 2, page 543). You can see that Edwards believed that man acted because of God's doing. The difference, on this issue, between Jonathan Edwards and Billy Graham is that Dr. Graham believes that man can do something, which will cause God to act. One reference in Scripture is sufficient to see who does what. "And a certain woman named Lydia, from the city of Thyatira, a seller of purple fabrics, a worshiper of God, was listening; and the Lord opened her heart to respond to the things spoken by Paul" (Acts 16:14). Read it slowly and notice who did what to make who believe what. It was not the gospel message that changed the heart of Lydia. It was not Lydia's faith that changed her heart. It was not a sinner's prayer that changed her heart. The Lord changed her heart, so that Lydia could believe the gospel. In addition, notice that she was "seeking" God before the Lord changed her heart.

God created us to worship Him. Invite unbelievers to church; then invite the church to worship, Bible study, prayer and fellowship. We cannot worship the Lord unless we love Him and obey His commandments. One commandment out of hundreds of His commandments is to "Make disciples of all nations . . . teaching them to observe all that I commanded you. . . ." (Matthew 28:19-20). To put it another way invite unbelievers into the true church. If the unbeliever professes faith, then disciple him or her with the basic doctrine of Scripture. It will reflect your love for God and His church.

The employment of two general principles will put the church into a biblical perspective: 1) Have special evangelistic meetings regularly, not just twice a year, and invite unbelievers to be the church; 2) Have worship services on the Lord's Day for the church according to the Word of God. There is no need to invite believers to church, because they are the church. Invite unbelievers into the church.

6. Is Communication Technology Good or Bad?

Technology, especially communications technology, popularized theological expression. Turn on the television and select your favorite preacher or Bible teacher. If one does not suit your individual preference, switch to another; there are hundreds available. Theological and academic credentials are no longer necessary to exegete the full counsel of God. All that is necessary is to have an "experience" with God. Diploma mills have risen to the occasion for those who want a theological degree without earning it. An uneducated, ill-equipped clergy, each generation growing exponentially with the expansion of communication technology, will result in an unhealthy church. The way to eliminate false doctrine is to, "Hold fast the pattern of sound words which you have heard from me [Paul], in faith and love which are in Christ Jesus" (2 Timothy 1:13). Then use technology to spread true doctrine.

Old Testament Israel has a notable resemblance to the New Testament Church; they are the people that belong to God. The Old Testament people of God had priests and prophets to lead in worship and teach the full counsel of God. After the death of Solomon, Jeroboam appointed himself as the leader of the people of God. What a mess! Jeroboam's unbiblical theology reminds me of cultural individualism and church autonomy. "And Jeroboam said in his heart, 'Now the kingdom may return to the house of David...'" (1 Kings12:26), but he didn't humble himself to realize "The heart is deceitful above all things, and desperately wicked..." (Jeremiah 17:9). Since Jeroboam did not know (very likely) or simply ignored the full counsel of God, he established his own place to worship and his own idols. Then he explained to the Old Testament church:

> It is too much for you to go up to Jerusalem. Here are your gods, O Israel, which brought you up from the land of Egypt! And he set up one in Bethel, and the other he put in Dan. Now this thing became a sin, for the people went to worship before

the one as far as Dan. He made shrines on the high places, and made priests from every class of people, who were not of the sons of Levi." (1 Kings 12:28-31)

Jeroboam interpreted or rather changed the Word of God to fit his agenda. The church followed him because he had become a celebrity among the people. A few words from that text stand out as a warning to those who profess the Christian religion: [Jeroboam] "made priests from every class of people, who were not of the sons of Levi." R. L. Dabney made the comment that "Jeroboam corrupted the religion of Israel partly by making priests of the lowest of the people" (*Discussions of Robert Lewis Dabney*, vol. 2, pg.69). Communication technology may be good or bad. It is good if the theology is faithful to the full counsel of God. It is bad if the theology is false.

7. Ministry of the Church

The mission of the church and the ministry of the church complement each other. The ministry of the church begins by "serving the Lord with all humility" (Acts 20:19). The servants of the Lord, (apostles, prophets, evangelists, pastors and teachers), are responsible for "equipping the saints for the work of ministry." The word "ministry" is derived from the word "minister" that literally means "to serve." The ministry of the church consists of serving in the body of Christ. Paul summarizes the ministry in his letter to the Ephesians.

Christ gave His church pastors and teachers to prepare God's people for works of service, so the mission of the church will be complete. Elders fill the office of the pastor and teacher. They are responsible for the oversight of the congregation. The Word of God defines this particular office.

> The elders who are among you I exhort, I who am a fellow elder and a witness of the sufferings of Christ, and also a partaker of the glory that will be revealed: Shepherd the flock of God which is among you, serving as overseers, not by compulsion but willingly, not for dishonest gain but eagerly; nor as being lords over those entrusted to you, but being examples to the flock. (1 Peter 5:1-4)

Pastors ought to have the gift of preaching and teaching. If the pastor has been faithful in his preparation, he ought to be able and willing to teach other pastors. Paul explains this concept to Timothy. "If you instruct the brethren in these things, you will be a good minister of Jesus Christ, nourished in the words of faith and of the good doctrine which you have carefully followed" (1 Timothy 4:6).

The role of the pastor is one of spiritual oversight. The role of the teacher is one skilled, able, and willing to teach the "good doctrine." There are two roles, but one office, the office of elder. The office of elder has taken a turn for the worse in recent centuries among evangelicals. The office holders have compromised their office, which will eventually cause the elder to abandon his biblical role.

I've studied and observed pastoral roles for nearly thirty years and conclude that the primary cause of the biblical pastor's disappearance is modernity. Modernity is a system produced by modernization and development. Modernity ultimately embraces relativism as the standard to interpret all of life. Since modernity has been a prevailing cultural philosophy, the roles of pastor and teacher take on worldviews occupied by the modern mind. In simple terminology, it is GIGO (garbage in – garbage out). This term was coined to explain how data input in a computer would ultimately be reflected in the output. If bad doctrine goes in, bad doctrine comes out. If good doctrine goes in, good doctrine comes out.

The pastor/teacher in the past was a church doctor, skilled in metaphysics, and the theologian in residence. His world and life view was rooted in the Word of God, not the words of men. There was a time when the pastor was truly a minister. Now the modern pastor is a CEO, a therapeutic counselor, and a management expert. There was a time when the pastor/teacher was educated in the classics, understood the historical philosophy of the culture, and respected in the community. Even though many hold a degree, they are un-educated and held in suspect by the world around them. The pastor/teacher was once a man of truth; now an irrational guru.

The pastors and teachers are the foundation for the ministry of the church, but the whole church must serve to build up the body of Christ. The pastors and teachers have the responsibility to prepare the saints for the mission and ministry of the church. Every Christian must be involved in the ministry of the church according to the gift Christ has given him or her. The elders of the church must identify the gifts of every individual. Then the elder's duty is to strengthen the gift in that person so the ministry will be complete. The perfection of the ministry of the church will be in the New Heavens and the New Earth.

Paul explains the tactics of the enemy that prevent the saints from participating in the ministry of the church. Paul says, "we should no longer be children, tossed to and fro and carried about with every wind of doctrine, by the trickery of men, in the cunning craftiness of deceitful plotting" (Ephesians 4:14). Avoid the tactics of the enemy and embrace the instruction from the Master by "speaking the truth in love" (Ephesians 4:15).

Is it possible that some particular churches have lost the ministry of the church? Is the foundation cracked and unstable? Have the gifts been absconded by the enemy? If so, then we should pray for the grace of repentance and recover the biblical ministry of the church.

8. Mission of the Church

The Latin word m*issio*, from which we get the English word mission, refers to "a sending forth." The Greek word *apostello*, from which we get the word apostle, refers to "one sent by authority of the sender to act on the senders behalf." The gospels and the Acts of the Apostles magnify the apostolic mission of the church (Matthew 28:18-20; John 17:6-18; Acts 13:1-3). The Lord Jesus Christ was sent on a mission and He sends His disciples on a mission. The two dimensions of the mission given by injunction are to make disciples and to teach the Word of God.

Evangelism is part of the process necessary to make disciples. However, instruction for the purpose of conversion is only one aspect of making disciples. Discipleship is an educational process. We are all disciples of one sort or another. A disciple is simply someone who learns from a teacher. In modern times, a disciple is a student. A Christian student is one who learns, believes, and practices the truth. Preaching the whole counsel of God is necessary for the convert to become a student. Christians are students of Jesus Christ by the means appointed by God. The two primary instruments include a curriculum and a teacher. The Bible is the curriculum and elders of the church are the teachers. The student of Jesus Christ through the means appointed must have the ability to receive the truth. Some people are able to receive the truth and some are not able to receive the truth (John 8:42-47). Discipleship is not mere mental assent to a system of doctrine. The disciple (student) will desire to put the truth into practice.

Evangelism is a Christian world and life view that embraces the good news of God's saving grace and sharing that good news with others. The evangelical church may have lost the biblical doctrine of evangelism to a man-designed doctrine of evangelism. A Scottish minister addressed this issue in the 19th century in a sermon to his congregation.

> It will be a sad day for our country if the men, who luxuriate in the excitement of man-made revivals, shall with their one-

sided views of truth, which have ever been the germs of serious errors, their lack of spiritual discernment, and their superficial experience, become the leaders of the religious thought and the conductors of religious movements...They may be successful in galvanizing, by a succession of sensational shocks, a multitude of dead, till they seem to be alive, and they raise them from their crypts, to take a place amidst the living in the house of the Lord; but far better would it be to leave the dead in the place of the dead, and prophesy to them there, till the living God himself shall quicken them. For death will soon resume its sway.

It is popular to admit people into the fellowship of the church and to the Lord's Table without any credible profession of faith, any understanding of the teaching of Christ, and no evidence of a true conversion.

It almost seems that some Christians believe and live as if the final purpose of the gospel is evangelization of the world. I do not believe the Bible teaches any such idea. Taking the gospel to a lost world is a duty for all Christians - a duty that must not be ignored on one hand, but on the other hand, evangelization must not become something Christians worship. Jesus said, "You shall be witnesses to Me...to the end of the earth" (Acts 1:8). Announcing the good news to the unbeliever is necessary to fulfill the mission of the church.

After His resurrection, Jesus appeared to a couple of His disciples. "Then He said to them, 'These are the words which I spoke to you while I was still with you, that all things must be fulfilled which were written in the Law of Moses and the Prophets and the Psalms concerning Me.' And He opened their understanding, that they might comprehend the Scriptures'" (Luke 24:44-45). This is a particularly powerful statement and the only one in the New Testament that mentions Jesus Christ as the focus in all three divisions of the Hebrew Bible. When Jesus spoke those words, He opened their understanding, that they might comprehend the Scriptures.

The composition of the teaching ministry of the church requires four components: The teacher, the student, the Word of God, and the Holy Spirit. If any of those are absent, the teaching ministry will not mature. Furthermore, the Christian will not know how to "observe all things that Christ commanded."

Every Christian is responsible and accountable before God to participate in the mission of the church. The mission should not be confused with the purpose or ministry of the church.

9. No Men In Israel

You may deny reality, but you cannot hide reality. Our nation is seriously divided along ethnic lines, economic factors, religious belief and many other world and life views. The marriage institution is the most dangerous division of all.

Marriage is a divine institution originating within God's covenant with man at creation. God ordained it in the perfect world before sin entered into the world. To understand this institution properly there are chronological factors that must be applied to the logic of the institution. Man, a male being, was created first. God created man to have dominion by the labor of his hands and the propagation of his own kind. Since man was alone, he had no mutual help to fulfill the covenant responsibilities God provided the woman, one of man's own kind, for mutual help.

God created a male and female human being that constitute a married couple (See Genesis 1:27). God's plan for marriage includes order and harmony. The Lord said, "I will make him a helper comparable to him" (Genesis 2:18). Although there are several renderings of the phrase "helper comparable to him," the essence of the text is that the woman is just right for the man. The woman made man complete.

After this remarkable creation, God brought the woman to man, thus forming the divine institution commonly known as marriage. Marriage is an ordinance of God's creative work. Marriage is not a sacrament and marriage, as an institution, does not belong to God's redemptive plan.

Now we have to ask: what happened to this divine institution? Sin entered the world. Sin does not change the fact that God ordained marriage and therefore God must regulate marriage. In fact, sin is all the more reason that marriage must be God regulated.

A careful examination of the Word of God will reveal the fundamental principles necessary for a biblical marriage and therefore a biblical family.

- Marriage is honorable. (Hebrews 13:4)
- The woman is necessary for the man. (Genesis 2 and 1 Corinthians 11:11-12)
- The man is the head in marriage. (1 Peter 3:1-7; Col. 3:18; Ephesians 5:22)

The honor and necessity of marriage is rarely questioned by any culture, because in most cultures males and females marry. In most cultures the government of the marriage is closely defined. In America, that is not the case.

The western culture has three kinds of government in the marriage:

- The husband is manager
- The wife is manager
- The husband and wife are co-managers

Which do you think is the Biblical form of marriage management? The model is the Holy Trinity - Father, Son, and Holy Spirit. In the Trinity, it is clear from the Bible that God the Father, God the Son, and God the Holy Spirit work in perfect harmony.

Unfortunately, when the husband does manage he often acts like a tyrant. A tyrant exercises authority, headship, and makes decisions, but what motivates the tyrant? Is it love or justice? The answer is no, no. A tyrant cannot exercise justice because he is motivated by his egocentricity. I expect much of male headship in the home is tyranny. The godly biblical prescription is dismissed as impossible in our permissive society. Feminism is the present day view of women ruling in the church and state. I'm not making any accusations because self-professing feminist claim feminism as their world view.

The authority of the man in a marriage relationship begins with the primary duty, which the Bible describes as love. Sentiment is not love. Sentiment is ones opinion or ones feeling toward someone else. Spontaneous sentiment is not biblical love. In a biblical marriage sentiment diminishes as love increases. The husband loves his wife with an overwhelming love and the wife submits to his godly leadership. Harmony and order prevail until the charm of Satan enters into the relationship.

The biblical illustration I use in my book, *The Dominant Culture*, may be helpful. The context is the nation of Israel during the period of the Judges.

The Bible states the children of Israel were harshly oppressed. During this oppression and suffering you would think that God would raise up a deliverer or a savior for the people. God raised up two deliverers, Othniel (Judges 3:9) and Ehud (Judges 3:15). When Ehud died the people of Israel, "did evil in the sight of the Lord."

Even though God's children were "harshly oppressed," the Bible does not mention their plea for help or that God raised up a deliverer. The Bible does not say that God raised Deborah to Judge Israel; it simply says, "Now Deborah, a prophetess, the wife of Lapidoth, was judging Israel at that time" (Judges 4:4). The nation of Israel found itself without a man as a Judge. The nation of Israel was uniquely a church/state ruled by God's appointed servants. The assertion that there were "no men in Israel" does not mean that some male human beings did not reside there, but the Bible makes it clear there was no male leadership in the church or the state.

The remedy for the breakdown of the biblical marriage institution is to follow the biblical principles for all of faith and practice. The great danger for our church and nation is "everyone did what was right in his own eyes." It is never too late to say, "we will follow the Lord."

10. Protestant Denominationalism

This title needs some explanation. The word protestant comes from the Latin word *protestari*, which has the root meaning "to protest." The Latin word *testari* means "to bear witness." The word "protestant" was used by the Christian church to describe those who protested the theology of the Roman Catholic Church in the 16th century. It became known as the Protestant Reformation.

Denominationalism relative to the Christian church describes a world view that designates names to various groups that are divided over biblical doctrine and theology. If the title describes the content of this article, then it must be a protest against a divided church. If the division is over biblical doctrine or theology, listen to the Word of God. "Now I plead with you, brethren, by the name of our Lord Jesus Christ, that you all speak the same thing, and that there be no divisions among you, but that you be perfectly joined together in the same mind and the same judgment" (1 Corinthians 1:10). Unfortunately, the sin nature will continue to denominate the visible church on earth.

Dr. Benard Ramm, a Baptist theologian, wrote an article nearly 45 years ago published in *Christianity Today* entitled "The Continental Divide in Contemporary Theology." He identified "three strands in contemporary theology" which were 1) the orthodox theology, which included all Protestant churches, 2) the modern theology, which included neo-orthodoxy, and 3) liberal theology. His final comment is worthy of attention. "Those who really know the cardinal doctrines of the Christian faith can differentiate the kind of theology which falls on the right side of this continental divide from that which falls on the wrong side."

Cardinal doctrines are the fundamental or basic doctrines of the Christian religion. The Devil is the great deceiver and along with the sin nature it is certain that the militant church on earth will not be un-denominated. However, every denomination of the Christian religion ought to have mutual agreement on the basics. The question is what defines the basics? I believe The Apostles' Creed is one of the best definitions of the cardinal doctrines. The traditional version used by the Western Church begins with "I believe." I prefer to use the collective version often used in the Eastern Church that begins with "we believe." The collective view is based on the fundamental teaching of Scripture. For instance, when Jesus taught the disciples to pray, He taught them to say "our" Father, not my Father and give "us" and forgive "us." Every denomination of Christians ought to be able to profess,

> We believe in God the Father almighty, maker of heaven and earth; and in Jesus Christ his only Son, our Lord; Who was conceived by the Holy Ghost, born of the Virgin Mary, suffered under Pontius Pilate, was crucified, dead and buried; He descended into hell; the third day he rose again from the dead; He ascended into heaven, and sitteth on the right hand of God the Father almighty; from thence He shall come to judge the quick and the dead. We believe in the Holy Ghost; the holy catholic church; the communion of the saints; the forgiveness of sins; the resurrection of the body; and the life everlasting. (*The Apostles' Creed*)

My prayer is that God will bring about a new reformation. My hope remains that the orthodox basic doctrine of Scripture will be recovered so the Protestant church may pursue the inspired apostle's challenge to be of "one mind."

11. Purpose of the Church

Biblical worship is the Christian response to God by recognizing and expressing God's worthiness because of His supreme worth. The full counsel of God reveals the primary purpose of the church of God is to worship the triune God. However, sinful man attributes too much worth to himself, which is a form of self-worship. It is also called idolatry or man-made worship.

It seems to me that many professing Christian worshippers are more interested in entertainment for themselves rather than worshipping the Lord God almighty. People love to worship according to their feelings. We live in an age when true worship has been replaced by entertainment of every sort. The application of managerial theory and the psychobabble theories are the great enemies of true biblical worship. Today the focus is on the worshipper rather than the object of worship, the true and living God. Idolatry in the modern evangelical church is rampant. The building where the church meets for worship is a popular object of worship, especially the multi-million dollar buildings. Music, drama presentations, and other performances have become objects of worship. Pastors, denominations, and church dogma are a few of the many idols found in the modern church. Restoring biblical worship ought to be the primary objective of every Christian.

A study of the full counsel of God is necessary to determine the outward expressions of worship. The debate is divided into two categories. The majority of Protestant churches assume the position that all expressions of worship are acceptable unless they are prohibited in Scripture. The minority report is that only the expressions commanded by God are acceptable. Although there are slight variations among the minority, they generally find prayer, offerings, singing Psalms and hymns, reading and preaching of the Word of God, the sacraments, and the benediction are necessary elements in public collective worship.

Worship to the true and living God is intended for believers who find joy in worship according to God's Word; therefore, unbelievers should not be invited to worship. A correct understanding of worship seems to escape from the minds of many Christians. Many times worship is a matter of self-satisfaction. The *Westminster Confession of Faith* teaches what the Bible teaches that true worship is God-centered worship. Religious worship is not something the worshipper receives; it is something the worshipper does. It is given to God, "not to angels, saints, or any other creature." Worship must be offered to the Father, the Son, and the Holy Spirit, to be equally adored and worshipped. Therefore, according to Westminster, only Christians may offer worship to God. Worship offered by unbelievers will not be acceptable to God and if Westminster is right, God will find worship by unbelievers despicable. Worship must be offered, not only to the triune God, but it must be offered through the Mediator, the Lord Jesus Christ. "There is one Mediator between God and man, the man Jesus Christ" (1 Timothy 2:5). After the fall and the entrance of sin to the created world and all its creatures, it makes sense that any religious worship is offered by sinful creatures. Therefore God only accepts "divine worship" through the sinless God-man the Lord Jesus Christ. The Lord himself said, "No one comes to the Father except through Me" (John 14:6). There is great comfort to Christians that their Mediator sacrificed Himself, understands their infirmities, and makes their worship acceptable to the triune God. For that reason a distinction should be made between a worship service for believers and an evangelistic service for unbelievers.

12. Theological Integrity

Since words are important, let me define theological integrity. It refers to the truth of God's nature and character and everything relative to the Lord, God almighty.

I have the same question for the church today that John Calvin had for the church over 400 years ago. "Do we hope for salvation from the gospel while no man is willing to run any risk in asserting its truth?" Calvin goes on to explain; "in so many cities and provinces the purity of Christianity is gone" (an excerpt from Calvin's treatise on *The True Method of Giving Peace*, and of *Reforming the Church*). I do not intend to speak against the Bride of Christ. However, I am concerned about the condition of the church for the sake of this and coming generations. To put this in proper perspective, I believe the evangelical church, including conservative Bible believing churches are in the process of slipping into a neo-dark age. I have argued that the church growth movement is the primary reason for this dilemma along with the children of modernity. Pragmatism, consumerism, relativism and a dozen other world and life views have contributed to this neo-dark age plague. The postmodern concept now contributes another dark side to this dilemma; the abandonment of truth. The church cannot ignore this exponential slippage because at the root of all these problems is theological integrity. Have I misunderstood our culture or is my understanding of church history clouded by my own subjective ideas? Even if I have, that will not change the verity of my fundamental argument that theological integrity is the root of all our church problems.

In another place John Calvin wrote,

> When Divine Truth is avowedly attacked, we must not tolerate the adulteration of one single iota of it. It is certainly not a trivial matter to see God's light extinguished by the devil's darkness; and besides, this matter is of greater moment than many suppose. Nor is it true, as they allege, that he who does

not acquiesce in the errors of others, shows deadly hate by dissenting from them.

Calvin's principle argument is as true today as it has been throughout the history of the church. Calvin was far more ambitious than we might anticipate in the church today. When theological integrity comes into the picture, it is foggy with feelings.

Theological integrity means that one vows (pledges, professes, or confesses) with a reasoning regenerated mind a belief system that works out consistently based on the Word of God. If your creedal statement(s) are the result of your understanding of the "full counsel of God" then your theological integrity will be demonstrated in human experience. It was theological integrity that brought Jesus to the point of a deadly confrontation with the right winged conservative religious leaders of his day (John 8:37-59). He even accused them of being children of the devil, the father of lies, so they must have been childish liars. A childish liar is the opposite of theological integrity. Those religious leaders were not able to understand the truth. That is precisely correct. They were unable to understand the truth, thus they could not believe the truth. Was the inability to understand truth a knowledge problem or was it a theological problem? It was both! Their wills were slaves to the devil (John 8:44). They were very willing to sacrifice theological integrity because of the condition of their souls. Their minds were clouded because of their sin nature. How sad that the Pharisees could not understand what Jesus meant when He said, "take heed that the light which is in you is not darkness" (Luke 11:35). Theological integrity means that you must have clear revelation and a clear mind (Ephesians 1:17).

The inspired, infallible and inerrant wisdom of Scripture posits: "A faithful witness does not lie, but a false witness will utter lies" (Proverbs 14:5). A lie is contrary to the truth. I just do not understand why Christians in general and church leaders in particular are so unconcerned about truth and ultimately theological integrity. The anti-confessional and anti-intellectual agendas are the primary agents leading the church away from theological integrity and into relativistic, humanistic, and pragmatic notions, all of which spell disaster for the future church.

Theological integrity is not the easy road. It was not easy for men like Martin Luther, John Calvin, Jonathan Edwards, or J. Gresham Machen. They suffered because theological integrity was important. In fact the Bible tells us that "all who desire to live godly in Christ Jesus will suffer persecution" (2 Timothy 3:12). If you are not suffering persecution perhaps, you do not desire to live godly in Christ Jesus. We must not forget that Jesus said, "you will be hated by all for My name's sake" (Matthew 10:22) and in another place Jesus said, "If they persecuted Me, they will also persecute you" (John 15:20). Theological integrity is not popular or attractive to the man-centered church growth movement, the broad evangelicals, or liberals, but theological integrity is necessary! Everyone will be held accountable on that day.

The genius of theological integrity is profoundly simple. The great 19th century theologian and church doctor James Henley Thornwell left these words for the church to ponder.

> We have minds that were made to know; we are constructed with a reference to truth and then reminds us not to turn "from the temple of truth to worship at the shrine of ignorance, error and shame... .This love of truth, which I have been endeavoring to recommend, will be the very last importance to you to guard you against the deceits of the world. . . .The world, the flesh and hell all conspire by glozing falsehood to seduce us to perdition. A covering is spread upon the grave and the pit, and the ways of sin are adorned with all that can please the eye, fascinate the ear or enchant the heart. Our security against these dangers is conviction for the truth." (*The Collected Writings of James Henley Thornwell*, vol. 2, p. 494-495)

My prayer is that God will raise up someone like Martin Luther, John Calvin, Jonathan Edwards, James Henley Thornwell, J. Gresham Machen or anyone willing to stand for theological integrity. My prayer is that the church will be reformed by the power of the Holy Spirit according to the Word of God. My prayer for the church is found in Psalm 25:21-22: "Let integrity and uprightness preserve me, for I wait for You. Redeem Israel, O God, Out of all their troubles!"

13. Assurance of Grace and Salvation (Part 1)

Believers have assurance of grace and salvation without having to see the death of the Lord Jesus Christ. The Word of God makes promises regarding assurance of salvation. However, deep down inside there may be the remnant of skepticism. Christians may ask, "how do I know I have assurance of salvation?" If the question infers the metaphysical (the existence that follows death), then we will find most everyone is a skeptic at some time or the other to some degree or the other.

With all the seriousness of life, death, and eternity, God's people should take pleasure in the doctrine of assurance. It is important to every Christian because the doctrine of assurance teaches that the Christian is in a state of grace and a favorable relationship with God. The doctrine of assurance is necessary to know and experience the certainty of the state of grace and the certainty of having a favorable relationship with God. The Bible teaches that evidence accompanies true assurance (Colossians 2:2). It is sad, but true that many professing Christians find false assurance in their own beliefs and their feelings based on human experience apart from the Word of God. Conjecture is never a reason to believe something is real. In the case of assurance of salvation, feelings and emotional sensations will never stand before the bar of eternal justice. The Bible teaches that many men deceive themselves into believing that they are in a state of grace and in a right relationship with God.

One Christian confession says that "hypocrites, and other unregenerate men, may vainly deceive themselves with false hopes and carnal presumptions" (*Westminster Confession of Faith*, 18.1). False assurance is less certain in the mind of many professing Christians than true assurance. It always has been. "Her heads judge for a bribe, her priests teach for pay, and her prophets divine for money, yet they lean on the Lord and say, is not the Lord among us? No harm can come upon us?" (Micah 3:11). False assurance was just as popular in the Old Testament as it is today.

True assurance does belong to those who "truly believe in the Lord Jesus, and love Him in sincerity, endeavoring to walk in all good conscience before Him" (*Doctrine of Sound Words*, by Martin Murphy, p. 109). The Bible asserts that Christians may know they have assurance. "These things I have written to you who believe in the name of the Son of God, that you may know that you have eternal life, and that you may continue to believe in the name of the Son of God" (1 John 5:13). When God renewed His covenant with the Israelites in the land of Moab God warned His people.

> So that there may not be among you man or woman or family or tribe, whose heart turns away today from the Lord our God, to go and serve the gods of these nations, and that there may not be among you a root bearing bitterness or wormwood; and so it may not happen, when he hears the words of this curse, that he blesses himself in his heart, saying, 'I shall have peace, even though I follow the dictates of my heart'—as though the drunkard could be included with the sober. (Deuteronomy 29:18-19)

It is sad indeed when people believe they have peace with God when in reality they are at war with God. The Lord Jesus Christ does not mince words on the issue of deceptive men who are without assurance of grace and salvation. The Lord said, "Beware of the false prophets, who come to you in sheep's clothing, but inwardly are ravenous wolves" (Matthew 7:15). False assurance will face reality because the Lord said, "Many will say to Me on that day, (the day of judgment) 'Lord, Lord, did we not prophesy in Your name, and in Your name cast out demons, and in Your name perform many miracles" (Matthew 7:22). The reference to "many" implies a large number. Also in the context of Matthew chapter seven, the large number refers to a large number in the church. The Words of Jesus Christ make it ring loud and clear that there is a large number in the church of Jesus Christ who are deceived in themselves. The words "false prophets" as Jesus used them does not merely refer to someone speaking of future events. In fact, a biblical prophet is someone who simply speaks forth. A false prophet is someone who speaks a lie with every intention to deceive and destroy with those lies. It is clear from the whole of Scripture that the false prophet is an enemy of God; therefore the false prophet is a man who is not in a state of grace or a favorable relationship with God. The false prophet has false assurance. On the day of judgment the Lord Jesus Christ, the Judge of heaven and earth will say, "I never knew you; DEPART FROM ME, you who practice lawlessness" (Matthew 7:23).

An atheist should expect to hear those words, but those who profess the Christian religion should not expect to hear those words, but as Jesus said, "many" will hear those words. To the professing Christian who is actually an unbeliever, those words from the mouth of Jesus Christ may seem harsh and unloving. To the professing believer who is actually a Christian, those words should simply be a reminder to examine their own condition before the final examination.

To say that a person can act wickedly, live a despicable life, and make mockery of the Word of God and still have assurance of grace and salvation is the most foolish of all thoughts. If professing Christians want to have assurance and confidence in God's saving grace, they must call out to God and say, "Teach me Your Word." If God provides the instruction and professing Christians do not listen, they should go the Lord and pray for His grace and mercy. If you belong to Jesus Christ you have every reason to have assurance of salvation and eternal life, because those reasons are found in the Word of God.

14. Assurance of Grace and Salvation (Part 2)

The largest part of the Christian church denies the doctrine of the assurance of salvation. It is at this point of Christian doctrine that the Roman Catholic Church and the Arminian branch of the evangelical church kiss and agree that Christians cannot have any certainty of their justification. According to the teaching of these churches, eternal life is only conditional. It makes perfectly good sense, because if an unbeliever can do something to save himself from eternal damnation, then surely the believer can do something to lose his right standing with God.

Christians have "an infallible assurance of faith founded upon the divine truth of the promises of salvation, the inward evidence of those graces unto which these promises are made, the testimony of the Spirit of adoption witnessing with our spirits that we are the children of God..." Fallible refers to something that may err or it may be false. Infallible is just the opposite; It will not err and will always be truthful.

One of the grounds of our assurance is the infallible truth and promise of salvation. Another ground of infallible assurance is the inward evidence of those graces unto which these promises are made. The inward evidence includes every aspect of sanctification and the spiritual maturity of the believer. The third ground of our assurance mentioned is the testimony of the Spirit of adoption witnessing with our spirits that we are the children of God. Again God speaks clearly that "he who believes in the Son of God has the witness in himself" (1 John 5:10). The final ground of assurance is the work of the Holy Spirit sealed unto the day of redemption. It must be remembered that feelings and emotions are not the grounds of assurance. However, an infallible assurance is not essential for salvation. In fact, it may be a lengthy struggle before the believer may obtain an infallible assurance that they are in a state of grace. It is the duty of every Christian to seek assurance through the right use of ordinary means such as attending the means of grace. Therefore, Christians will be diligent to make their calling and election sure. The duty must likewise be accompanied by the right disposition of the heart reflected by the fruit coming from assurance. Assurance of salvation is not accompanied by presumptive regeneration.

Christians are subject to question their assurance of salvation because experience does not always match the doctrine they believe. The Bible is clear about the faith and salvation of the elect. It is impossible to lose faith and salvation, but one may lose assurance of faith and assurance of salvation. The believer will never lose his or her salvation having received the effectual call.

Neglect and disregard for God's justice, love and mercy (Micah 6:8) often accompanies prosperity and blessing. Such was the case with Israel in the Old Testament and the ultimate downfall first of the northern kingdom and finally the southern kingdom. Temptation that leads to some grievous sin or even a minor omission like failing to study the Bible and pray may be reflected in the absence of assurance. However, in due time the assurance may return. Until assurance once again belongs to the believer they are supported from utter despair. The believer will remember that Christ is not only our Savior he is our Lord, the same yesterday, today, and forever.

15. Be a Friend of God

When King Jehoshaphat was in despair he cried out to God saying "Didst Thou not, O our God, drive out the inhabitants of this land before Thy people Israel, and give it to the descendants of Abraham Thy friend forever?" Abraham had a unique standing with God; God's friend forever. In the New Testament James confirms the Old Testament passage by saying that Abraham was called a friend of God.

God created man to enjoy and fellowship with, but man failed God in the covenant promise. God gave man a good place to live – the Garden of Eden. God gave man good water and food and he gave man a good job tending the garden. A good God to the man he created. God instructed man not to do one thing, which is what I mean by a covenant relationship. Man disobeyed God and the favorable covenant relationship was broken.

Some historians estimate that during the past 5000 yrs. over 8000 covenants have been made and broken between nations. The average time they remained in force was two years. The number of wars that resulted was 14,531 and 364,000,000 people were killed. God made a covenant with mankind during the creation order and I believe it remains in effect to this day. By all rights God should have destroyed the human race, which would have served justice, but God had compassion on the sinful race and let them live with a promise of hope and redemption. The Bible explains:

> For you know that it was not with perishable things such as silver and gold that you were redeemed from the empty way of life handed down to you from your forefathers, but with the precious blood of Christ, a lamb without blemish or defect. He was chosen before the creation of the world, but was revealed in these last times for your sake. Through him you believe in God, who raised him from the dead and glorified him, and so your faith and hope are in God. (1 Peter 1:18-20)

From these verses Christians find the assurance that God's plan from eternity past is effective in the present day. The Bible teaches that God sent forth His Son in order that He might redeem those who were under the Law, that we might receive the adoption as sons and receive the Spirit of His Son in our hearts. When God adopts a son (or a daughter) it is a permanent relationship. It is then that you become a friend of God forever. Christian friends, we are to rejoice in knowing that we are friends of the creator of the Universe. If God be with us we shall never be alone, nor shall we feel lonely. If God be with us, He will not be inactive on our behalf. He will provide for us so that we shall not be needy or destitute. He will preserve us so that we shall not perish. There is an old English proverb that says, "He cannot be poor who has the Lord Mayor for his uncle."

We may rather say, "He cannot be poor who has God for his friend." The Psalmist surely knew what friendship with God was like when he said, "I have been young and now I am old; Yet I have not seen the righteous forsaken, or his descendants begging bread."

16. Biblical Interpretation Under Siege

Preaching and teaching false doctrine is a means of spiritual death. Jesus said, "If the blind leads the blind, both will fall into a ditch" (Matthew 15:14). If preachers and teachers use the allegorical method they will meet the same destiny. Unfortunately many, if not most preachers, use allegorical biblical interpretation. Using this method the interpreter seeks to find a "deeper" or "spiritual" meaning in a text. The Greek word *allegoria* may be literally translated as "speaking one thing, but signifying something else." The allegorical method is explicitly found in Galatians 4:24 where Paul speaks allegorically saying: "for these women are two covenants, one proceeding from Mount Sinai bearing children who are to be slaves; she is Hagar." The misuse of the allegorical method is common and leads to multiple meanings of Scripture. The allegorical method should be used with the greatest of care with the most skilled of godly men engaged in the interpretation of Scripture.

I use the *grammatico-historical* method of interpretation. It is used to determine the intended meaning of words in Scripture. The question must be asked: what did the writer intend to say? Words in Scripture are to be taken literally unless they are obviously figurative. The history (context) of Scripture must be considered in biblical interpretation. The goal is an objective understanding of the Word of God.

Exegesis refers to using the proper tools and instruments to discover and understand the true meaning of any biblical text. Therefore, the Bible is interpreted and explained. The meaning of the biblical text, which has one meaning, is then applied to any given situation. The pastor must know and practice sound exegesis to properly equip the congregation for works of service.

The "analogy of faith" is a phrase used for biblical interpretation according to the 16th century Reformers. It states that difficult passages of Scripture must be interpreted in light of other clear passages. This fundamental principle of the sixteenth century Reformation acknowledges "Scripture alone" as the basic doctrine of

Protestant Christianity. The rejection of "Scripture alone" was the primary irresolvable division between the Roman Catholic Church and the Protestant Church.

Christian pastors and teachers should teach the simple principles of hermeneutics. If they don't know the principles of biblical interpretation, they should not be pastors and teachers. Hermeneutics deals with rules of exegesis and its purpose is to understand the intended meaning of a communication, especially the Bible.

The postmodern concept denies absolute truth. The influence has been profound and has caused more than a few professing Bible scholars to deny portions of Scripture because it is deemed relative to the culture of origination. The argument goes something like this: "Such and such biblical text was relative to the period in which Jesus lived, but it does not apply to our culture."

The reason there are hundreds of denominations and thousands of disenfranchised professing Christian congregations is because they cannot agree on the interpretation of Scripture. The Bible is true or false; When Bible doctrine is interpreted it will be true doctrine or false doctrine. Playing Russian Roulette with interpretative theory may end in an unfavorable relationship with God.

17. Broken Promises

Anyone may read this article, but only Christians who believe the Bible is the ultimate authority in life will truly believe it and embrace it. The bulk of this article was taken from my commentary on chapter 22, "Oaths and Vows," of the *Westminster Confession of Faith*. My motivation for writing on this subject is the blatant disregard that high profile professing Christian politicians have for keeping promises. However, it applies to every individual Christian.

The word "promise" corresponds to words like covenant, oath, and vow. An oath is voluntary, but the ninth commandment, "you shall not lie" is fundamental to the execution of the oath. When an oath is made the one who swears the oath calls on God as his witness. Since God cannot err in relation to truth, the party making the oath calls on God to judge him or her. Making a promise to God as a witness leaves an awesome responsibility on the shoulders of the one swearing the oath. One must be careful not to swear an oath of perpetuity. When someone says, "I will remain till death do us part" there is no way out. Making frivolous statements and promises is a sin, a violation of the ninth commandment, not only to the person affected by the lie, but also to God who was a witness to it. I'm seventy one years old and for half of those years I was agnostic toward Christianity. I expected people to lie and break promises. When I was converted to Christianity, I thought Christians would be truthful. During the past thirty-five years, I've experienced more lies and broken promises from Christians than I did from my pagan past.

If the *Westminster Confession of Faith* was correctly interpreted based on the teaching of the Bible then God is called upon to judge whether or not the promise was honorable and truthful. *Westminster* defines a vow, "of the like nature with a promissory oath." Since a promissory note generally describes a promise to pay a fixed sum on a fixed day, it must be concluded that vows must be taken seriously with resulting consequences. However, the risk of consequences should in no way inhibit one from making vows to God. Once the commitment is made it must be kept or otherwise it is a sin against

God. "When you make a vow to God, do not be late in paying it, for He takes no delight in fools. Pay what you vow" (Ecclesiastes 5:4).

The *Westminster Confession of Faith* was drafted and approved at a time when objective and absolute truth was not in question. By the end of the 20th century, there was no consensus that truth actually existed independent of the human brain. It is interesting that *Westminster* posits that one must be "fully persuaded" or completely convinced. Full persuasion for the Christian brings a heavy responsibility, because God hates liars. "Speak each man the truth to his neighbor . . . and do not love a false oath, for all these are things I hate Says the Lord" (Zechariah 8:16-17). In his commentary on the 9th commandment, Thomas Watson said, "How can you converse or bargain with a man when you cannot trust a word he says? This sin highly provokes God. Ananias and Sapphira were struck dead for telling a lie."

No man should make an "oath to anything but what is good and just, and what he believes so to be, and what he is able and resolved to perform." To break an oath makes one a liar. Jesus associates liars with the Devil (John 8:44), so professing Christians should be very careful not to say something they cannot do or say something that is not true.

God will not be a witness to cunning, deceitful, dishonest, and evasive language. God knows the heart, regardless of what comes out of the mouth. God will not tolerate equivocation. In logic, equivocation may be the bad use of English, which is a result of ignorance.

However, equivocation may be used to deceive by using a word or phrase that could take two different meanings. *Westminster* has the latter in mind. It is possible for a Christian to say technically "I meant such and such," but in the heart he may intend to convey the opposite meaning. The 17th century Reformer, Francis Turretin, rightly states, "an oath ought to be an end of all controversy according to the apostle (Hebrews 6:16), but where there is equivocation, controversies are rather multiplied than ended" (*Institutes of Elenctic Theology*, Vol. 2, p. 66ff).

The Word of God is very clear on this doctrine: "May it never be! Rather, let God be found true, though every man be found a liar, as it is written, 'That Thou mightest be justified in Thy words, and mightest prevail when Thou art judged'" (Romans 3:4). An oath "binds to performance, although to a man's own hurt." It is very common for people to make promises and then break them if the oath is to their disadvantage. An oath may be broken only if it is a sin to keep it. Mental reservations will not save the party making the oath, because God will judge the heart. "With his mouth one speaks peace to his neighbor, but inwardly he sets an ambush for him" (Jeremiah 9:8; 2 Corinthians 4:2).

I conclude the dreadful subject with a few comments from the mind of God through the mouth of Jeremiah the prophet. The historical context is prior to and during God's judgment falling on Jerusalem and God's people (586 B.C.).

> Jeremiah 5:21 – Hear this now O foolish people, without understanding, who have eyes and see not and who have ears and hear not.

> Jeremiah 5:31 – The prophets prophesy falsely; And the priests rule by their own power; And My people love to have it so.

> Jeremiah 7:10 – Truth has perished and has been cut off from their mouth.

In summary, those who professed to be God's people in Jerusalem (Now the church) were under the influence of false teaching and man-made doctrine and the people loved it.

The remedy: Return to the Lord. Jesus will never lie or break a promise because He is the way, the truth, and the life.

To swear an oath or to take a vow is the same as making a promise; to break a promise makes a person a liar. Jesus associates liars with Satan because "Satan is a liar and the father of it" (John 8:44). The excuses I've heard from the mouth of liars are many.

1. It was just a little white lie.
2. I know I made a promise, but I forgot.
3. I know what I said, but I really didn't mean it.
4. Preaching and teaching false doctrine is not a lie.

Those are just a few of the many excuses. However, a lie is a lie.

I try to be generous by providing free copies of my books. It is my ministry. Sometimes I give them away, no strings attached. Other times I give a copy of a book with a request for a brief review posted on Amazon (most of them are to pastors or church leaders). The majority of them accept the complimentary copy and promise to post a review, but most of them never post a review. I've had more broken promises on other issues than I can count.

Broken promises in the institution of marriage are frequent and permanent. I always referred to the marriage ceremony as the marriage covenant. It always included the following:

> Marriage is a divine ordinance instituted at creation for man's happiness and God's glory. The sacredness of the relation is revealed by the fact that the Holy Spirit has selected it as an emblem of the union existing between our Lord and His bride, the Church.
>
> The inseparable union of Christ to His Bride, the Church, indicates the permanence of this marriage covenant.
>
> In connection with this union there are certain qualities that should characterize your marriage.
>
> If it be your intention to take each other as husband and wife, you will demonstrate this by uniting your right hands.
>
> Do you, (Man's Name), take (Woman's Name), whom you now hold by the hand to be your lawful and wedded wife, and do you promise in the presence of God and these witnesses to be to her a faithful, loving and devoted husband, so long as you both shall live?
>
> Do you, (Woman's Name), take (Man's Name), whom you now hold by the hand to be your lawful and wedded husband and do you promise in the presence of God and these witnesses to be to him a faithful, loving and obedient wife, so long as you both shall live?

Let these rings be the token of your plighted faith, and the memorial of your mutual and unending love for each other.

(Man) and (Woman), you have pledged your love to each other in the presence of almighty God and of these witnesses, and have sealed your solemn marital vows with the giving and receiving of these rings.

May it please God to place the seal of His loving approval upon the union of these two hearts and lives in the sacred bonds of matrimony. Go to God regularly asking for enabling grace so that you may keep the vows you have just made.

Whether in prosperity or in adversity, in sickness or in health, in sorrow or in joy, remember the vows you have just made.

The marriage covenant was God's idea, not man's. And just as God provided Eve for Adam, God has provided (Woman) for (Man). God has brought them together "therefore what God has joined together, let not man separate."

Is there a remedy for broken oaths, vows, and promises? It is: FORGIVENESS, REPENTANCE, and RECONCILIATION. Consider life without the remedy! Without forgiveness it is hell. Jesus said: "He who is of God hears God's words; therefore you do not hear, because you are not of God" (John 8:47).

18. Who Is Independent?

Just before the 4th of July each year television, radio, newspapers, internet and literally every form of communication writes or talks about celebrating Independence Day. It is my belief that Christians around the world ought to celebrate dependence day. These are a few thoughts to ponder relative to this important concept, commonly called independence. As a national holiday, Independence Day, is the occasion to celebrate the absolved relationship between the 13 confederated colonies and the throne of Great Britain. The despotic and tyrannical rule of King George III provoked the colonies to dissolve the relationship.

It is said that Thomas Jefferson was primarily responsible for drafting the declaration of independence. Thomas Jefferson's individualism is probably responsible for his use of the word independent. You will not have to put forth much effort to discover the truth about Thomas Jefferson. He denied the authority of Scripture, the deity of Christ, and God's spiritual nature. In a letter to John Adams, Aug. 15, 1820 Jefferson said:

> To talk of immaterial existences is to talk of nothings. To say that the human soul, angels, god, are immaterial, is to say they are nothings, or that there is no god, no angels, no soul. I cannot reason otherwise: but I believe I am supported in my creed of materialism by Locke, Tracy, and Stewart. At what age the Christian church adopted this heresy of immaterialism, this masked atheism, crept in, I do not know.

For Jefferson, the existence of God equals nothing. Jefferson's religion was individualism. Jefferson's individualism emerged to become one the most prominent religious views in western civilization. The formula for its success has an American and European contribution. From the American Revolution came "life, liberty, and the pursuit of happiness." From the French Revolution came "liberty, equality and fraternity." Jefferson's declaration says

"We hold these truths to be self-evident that all men are created equal, that they are endowed by their creator with certain unalienable rights, that among these are:

1) Life
2) Liberty
3) Pursuit of happiness

Christian people practically ignore Christian theology when national patriotism is mentioned. What Thomas Jefferson didn't realize is that an independent God gave the words life, liberty, happiness, equality and fraternity to dependent people. An individual or a nation will not acquire them without the generous hand of God.

Individualism is the predominant religion in the United States. This destructive religious view comes couched in terms like individual freedom and independence. It stresses the worth of self and individual ability to engage in political, social, and religious life. The individualistic independent worldview produces a democracy. Democracy literally means people rule. Democracy stands in opposition to theocracy. Democracy means "people rule" and theocracy means "God rules." Is any person independent or any nation independent? The answer is no! God alone is independent. All existing matter depends on God's independent being.

Am I advocating that the United States stop the great celebration every 4th of July? No! If I had been alive during the revolutionary war, I would have supported the separation from the tyranny of an ungodly ruler like King George. I would have called it separation from the British Throne day. I would also call for another celebration. "Dependence on God Every day and forever" which if put into practice would insure freedom from tyranny in the right sense. Paul told the philosophers at Athens what the people in the United States need to hear: "In Him we live and move and have our being" (Acts 17:28).

The Bible paints a vivid picture of man's dependence on God. The spirit of individualism posits, "I am" but God declares "I am!" Babylon, the great nation that ruled the world during the reign of Nebuchadnezzar believed in the religion of individualism. A good example of the "I am" religion is found in the book of Isaiah. The king of Babylon cried out what most people keep to themselves; "I am and there is no one else besides me" (Isaiah 47:10). It is the pinnacle of sinful human arrogance and the core of the sin nature.

How many times have I heard people, professing Christians, say "pray that God will bless America?" Why not pray "God bless Iran, Afghanistan, and India? These countries need God to visit them with His grace and mercy just as He did the 13 states that originally formed a confederation, but later a federation, commonly called the United States, however un-United they may be today.

The Bible is replete with words describing God as the only independent, necessary self-existent being. While King Nebuchadnezzar was flaunting his independence, God said to him, "King Nebuchadnezzar, to you it is declared: sovereignty has been removed from you, and you will be driven away from mankind, and your dwelling place will be with the beasts of the field. You will be given grass to eat like cattle, and the seven periods of time will pass over you, until you recognize that the Most High is ruler over the realm of mankind, and bestows it on whomever He wishes" (Daniel 4:31-32).

Every person will have to decide whether to celebrate the independence of God or the independence of self, or the independence of the United States. The only way to celebrate the independence of God requires an understanding of His nature and character. Some things like independence belong to God and to Him alone.

Another aspect of His being is simplicity and unity. God is not a compound being with various parts. It is a theological truth that has practical applications. There will be millions upon millions people who may otherwise believe in God, yet on the 4th of July they will steal a portion of God's unique character, his independence, and give it to the people that govern the United States.

Before I explain how that will happen, it will be necessary for us to affirm the independence of God. Then we affirm His unity. The Bible says, "God is spirit" therefore, unlike humans He is not a composition of parts. God is one God. He is incapable of being divided into parts. Every nation is "divisible," but God's kingdom cannot be divided. Unfortunately many professing Christians try to rob God of His unique character. I am as guilty as anyone because I said it so many times when I recited the pledge of allegiance: "one nation indivisible."

Please for the sake of truth and sanity, stop and meditate on the word "indivisible." Every nation on this planet is divisible. Every material substance is capable of division. Even the atom is divisible, even though it cannot be cut into pieces. God and God alone is indivisible. The independence and simplicity of God are not merely caricatures that misrepresent who He is. They are very real, but Christians often fail to recognize them.

Words have lost much ground in the wake of a culture that has crowned as the queen, "image is everything." Words like independence, indivisibility, and united in a culture that is absolutely dependent and remarkably divided does not make sense. This country is divided by religious faith: Protestant, Catholic, Baptist, Methodist, Presbyterian, et al. This country is divided politically: Republican and Democratic parties and many more. This country is divided over social issues that consist of a long list of cultural wars: Abortion, Law, and Education, et al.

Many evangelicals believe that Christianity has lost its influence in the United States. I interpret that to mean God's blessing has departed. It is not so much that God has departed. God has simply allowed the worldview known as individualism to rule in the land. It is as if God said, "You want to do it your way, have at it."

The doctrine is clear, the application is overwhelming, and so what shall we do? The answer is simple. Do what the Lord said to the nation of Israel (now the church) many times over for nearly 600 years of their history: "Return to the Lord!" The Church is commanded by the Word of God, to return to the Lord. The Bible never commands the nation, commonly known by the term "United States" to return to the Lord. However, the Bible commands the church to "make disciples of all nations." The Church ought to prevail in the culture with biblical worldviews. Returning to the Lord is something the Church should do every day so the Church may engage in the culture (the nation) every day. The first place to start is to know the Lord. He has revealed Himself in His Word. Re-discover His nature and character. Admit that God is independent and all creation is dependent.

The first necessary step to overcome the Jeffersonian individualism and return to God is with the recognition that God actively provides for His creation. Eighteenth century Deism argued in favor of the generous providence of God, but denied God's personal involvement. The deist said God is not active in the universe, especially among individual people. God created natural laws that give us life, liberty, and the pursuit of happiness. The deist claims those laws regulate life, not God's active hand.

Today every rational creature in this nation ought to celebrate God's generous providence. They ought to say this is the day that we depend on God for life and all the joy associated with God's blessing. The doctrine of God's sovereignty replaces individualism.

> Psalm 103:19 – The Lord has established His throne in heaven, and His kingdom rules over all
>
> Job 12:23 – He makes nations great and destroys them; He enlarges nations, and guides them.

The Bible explains God's providence in terms of His 1) sustenance   2) government   3) provision and   4) concurrence.

> 1) <u>Sustenance</u> - What God creates He sustains. He holds all things together. The universe and everything within it is dependent upon the being and power of God for continuity of existence as well as origin of existence. The Universe was not created and left like a clock ticking away to the point of expiration, as many deists believe.
>
> 2) <u>Government of God</u> - God is the Supreme Governor who rules the world because of his absolute authority and power to govern. When King Nebuchadnezzar came to his senses he said that: God's dominion is an everlasting dominion; His Kingdom endures from generation to generation; His government is the directing and disposing of all things that come to pass. The adversarial disposition of man is to reject the government of God. Man rejects absolute authority. Man

rejects the power of God. Common sense and the Bible tell us to respect the government of God because He provides.

3) <u>Provision</u> - God, whose foreseeing of all things is based on His foreordination of all things, is the provider who prepares a future for His people. Not only prepares a future, but meets all their needs. God provided the ultimate need of His people by sending His only Son to redeem His people. The ultimate provision was the substitutionary atonement to satisfy the wrath of God. The biblical pattern is that the Lord provides and His people are grateful.

One concept of God's providence is often overlooked.

4) <u>Concurrence</u> – God brings His plan to pass by His sovereignty through human means. For example, the sons of Israel sold Joseph into slavery. Later Joseph explained: And as for you, you meant evil against me, but God meant it for good in order to bring about this present result, to preserve many people alive" (Genesis 50:20). "And we know that God causes all things to work together for good to those who love God, to those who are called according to His purpose" (Romans 8:28).

Christians ought to take first things first. Do not undertake the study of any field of science until the nature and character of God is understood, believed, and defended.

His Sovereignty
His independence
His simplicity and unity
His eternality
His perfections
His goodness
His truth
His holiness

King of kings and Lord of lords is a statement of God's sovereignty. Every king, president, governor, ruler and any other person in authority is subordinate to the great King and Lord of heaven and earth. They all depend on the sovereign King and Lord God Almighty. He has brought down rulers from their thrones" (Luke 1:52).

On the 4th of July celebrate dependence day and the freedom we enjoy in the United States because of God's generous providence.

19. Christmas (Part 1)

Millions upon millions of people will celebrate a national holiday on December 25th each year. It is commonly referred to as Christmas. Some people describe this season of the year in terms of the "winter holiday madness."

It is with sadness that the incarnation of Jesus Christ is described by madness. The incarnation of Christ means He came in the "likeness of men." The holiday season ought to be festive. However, it has been overtaken with Christmas madness. I hope Christians everywhere will seek personal reformation from the Word of God, so that the mind of Christ will prevail in discerning the difference in the incarnation of Christ and the winter holiday madness.

Christmas is a timeless celebration; Jesus Christ is God, the second person of the Trinity. Christ is the exact representation of God's nature according to the writer of Hebrews. "Christ is the image of the invisible God" (Colossians 1:15). This is a most profound concept, because it is truly the message of Christmas. The intended occasion for Christmas was to emphasize the birth of Jesus Christ or to put it another way Christmas was the celebration of God, the second person of the Trinity, taking to himself a true body and a reasonable soul. It is properly called the incarnation of Jesus Christ. The incarnation of Jesus Christ means that a heavenly Reality becomes an earthly Reality.

Christmas is an everyday event for Christians because it reminds them to worship Jesus Christ. They worship Him because He is the exact representation of the living God, not in body but in essence.

> The essence of Jesus Christ is reality.
> We worship Jesus Christ.
> Therefore we worship reality, not some imaginary form.

The church has abused the nature of Jesus Christ who is the very image of God. Jesus Christ has been and is the most misunderstood figure throughout human history, because they have not seen the image of the invisible God. They have not seen the reality of the God-man. Christians must go beyond the physical image for their hope. They go to the image of the invisible God for their eternal hope.

The real question is: What image do you have of Jesus Christ? What does the image of the invisible God mean to you?

> Is he a kind and gentle man?
> Is he a man who heals your sickness?
> Is he the one who provides financially?
> Is he your savior?

Too often Christians think that way. That is a poor image of Jesus Christ. Although He may be all those things, they do not represent His essence and nature. The Christmas challenge is to see Jesus Christ in His fullness.

We can begin to discern the image of the invisible God by considering the threefold work of Jesus Christ as the Prophet, Priest, and King.

As a prophet He revealed to the church the whole will of God in things concerning salvation and edification. He is the prophet par excellence - Listen to His words and obey him.

As a priest He appeared in the presence of God to satisfy God's wrath against the sinner. He is the heavenly High Priest - Let Him be your Mediator and the one who stands in your behalf.

As a king He is the sovereign head of the church. He rules over His kingdom with eternal power and authority. You are expected to worship and adore your king.

We see images of Jesus Christ at every juncture during the Christmas season, but many of them do not represent the essence of His substance in reality. They are false images. We must replace those false images with the true image of Jesus Christ. I suggest you take time to retreat from the madness of this holiday season and muse the perfections of Jesus Christ.

One day every person will meet, face to face, the image of the invisible God. On that day Christians will see the infinite and eternal loveliness of Jesus Christ. On that day Christians will see an unchangeable image of the invisible God.

Christians should use this national holiday to share the true image of Jesus Christ. Take this opportunity to worship the Christ of Christmas.

Everyone has a different need, but I expect every Christian or unbeliever wants peace. Peace within and peace among men and nations no doubt lies at the root of our existence. During this "winter holiday madness" listen to hymns like:

> O Come, O Come, Emmanuel
> -Fill all the world with heaven's peace,
>
> It Came upon the Midnight Clear
> -Peace on the earth
>
> Hark! The Herald Angels Sing
> -Hail the heaven born Prince of Peace
>
> O Little Town of Bethlehem
> -peace to men on earth
>
> Sleep in heavenly peace

Jesus Christ is peace. The supremacy of His incarnation is the message I have during the "winter holiday madness.

20. Christmas (Part 2)

'Twas the night before Christmas or was it two nights before Christmas? What difference does it make anyhow, we all know the story. As a matter of fact it seems that Christmas is full of stories. For instance, there are a few who still tell the story about Jesus Christ and his birth at Bethlehem. Now that is an interesting story. It is the story about the incarnation of Jesus Christ.

The incarnation (the Latin phrase, *in carne* means "in flesh") is a concept that describes the union of the second person of the Trinity, Jesus Christ, to a true body and a reasonable soul. The 17th century Westminster Assembly asked the question, "How did Christ, the Son of God, become man?" They answered the question: "Christ, the Son of God, became man by assuming a real body and a reasoning soul. He was conceived by the power of the Holy Spirit in the womb of the Virgin Mary, who gave birth to Him; yet He was sinless." The result was the joining of the metaphysical to the physical, yet both maintain the essential characteristics of their nature. *Vere homo* (fully and truly man) and *vere deus* (fully and truly God) is how the early church fathers described this union of God and man, because the Latin word *vere* represents absolute truth. If this is beginning to sound complicated, it is the fault of the church, because the church has passed on neat little stories instead of substantive teaching on this wonderful event that is part of the salvation story. We are challenged to a full orbed investigation of the person of Jesus Christ. The Christmas story is full and rich as it describes how the eternal Word became flesh and lived among men.

The 20th century church is fractured and in a state of tumultuous disorder as it tries to tell the Christmas story. The story has so many versions. The problem is so vast it could not be contained in one single book, but in summary the problem is at least four-fold.

First, the controverted mystery of the birth of Christ is resolved by correctly understanding the role of Scripture in explaining the birth of Jesus Christ. Yes, a mystery, but yes the mystery is believable by overwhelming biblical evidence and the power of the Holy Spirit residing in the soul. The Christmas celebration is a time when Christians can focus on the believable, but mysterious birth of the Lord Jesus Christ.

Second, theological liberalism has reduced the miracle of the incarnation (the union of God and man) to "God incognito in Jesus" according to Dr. David Wells a distinguished professor at Gordon-Conwell Theological Seminary. Wells, a conservative theologian, states the error of theological liberalism without apology. To think that God is unknown in the historical person of Jesus Christ turns the Christmas story into an ordinary birth of an ordinary man.

Third, another distortion of the Christmas story emerges from privatized religion. Christians have allowed the democratic process to destroy the concept of kingship. Christianity in the United States has been democratized so that biblical interpretation is every individual's right. The Bible does not allow for self-rule (privatized religion). The birth of Jesus Christ is the story of the birth of a king, a king who still rules today. The Kingdom of God is ruled by a King; His name is King Jesus.

Fourth, the disagreement about the meaning of the "two natures" of Jesus Christ (fully God and fully man) has profoundly affected the understanding or misunderstanding of the Christmas story. Christmas is a good time for Christians to apprehend a correct understanding of the person and nature of Jesus Christ. Unfortunately, many church leaders will replace sound teaching with a musical concert.

Much of the false doctrine in the Christian religion began with an unbiblical view of the nature of Jesus Christ. It often begins when one tries to make Jesus Christ more or less of a human being than He really is, or tries to add or take away from His divine nature. The arguments will not be settled any time soon because the church has neglected to consistently, courageously, and compellingly tell the story of Jesus Christ.

The story of Jesus Christ is the story about the only begotten Son of God who took to Himself the human nature. Even so, Jesus Christ remained and still remains the very and eternal God. He is of the same substance and equal to God the Father. It is the story about the God-man with two whole, perfect, and distinct natures. This is a wonderful story to tell, because this is an eternal story.

There are many other problems that distort the story of Jesus Christ, but Christians can rejoice, if they tell true story of the birth of Jesus Christ.

21. Disappearance of Ultimate Authority

I have a few words relative to the disappearance of the once strong evangelical church. Then I came to my senses and realized that virtually no one, hyperbolically speaking, believes the 16th century evangelical church is disappearing. The "church" (tongue and cheek) is a prosperous economic machine managed by people who are alleged faithful men. Money management is their specialty. The CEO's are professional sophists; they tell people that part of the truth that is not offensive. They are celebrities in their own right.

However, the time has arrived and some of the most prominent professing evangelicals "will not endure sound doctrine, but according to their own desires, because they have itching ears, they will heap up for themselves teachers; and they will turn their ears away from the truth, and be turned aside to fables" (2 Timothy 4:3-4). So it was easy for me to be convinced to change direction and discuss the disappearance of ultimate authority in the once strong evangelical church.

For the sake of all those who are in the womb of their mothers and the young children who will have to live in a postmodern culture you should weigh carefully the concept of constitutional authority. There must be an objective standard, since human rulers are sinful and corrupt. The authority given human rulers is given by God, the Lord of all history and nations. The abuse of authority is tyranny. I'll let you decide if you feel tyrannized because of the abuse of authority from the hands of government leaders.

The effects of despotic power, guided and inflamed by the lust for power will oppress and finally imprison people like the nation Israel was oppressed and in bondage first to the Egyptians and then to the Babylonian government. Their suffering was the fruit of their ignorance of authority and submission to it. When King Nebuchadnezzar invaded the land of Judea, it was devastating for the people of God to be carried away in bondage. The Hebrew nation suffered the indignity because they rejected the ultimate authority of God.

The Hebrew nation was given a form of government over which God Himself was the Governor and King. It was a form of government with an objective standard that assured justice without oppression and tyranny. The people agreed with the law and freely adopted it. Then on occasions they would renew their covenant with God. The constitution they adopted, heavenly as it was, with all the promises of peace and prosperity, soon went by the wayside. They demanded a king, like the nations around them. They were not happy with their constitution, even though it came to them by ultimate authority. If we do not submit to the ultimate authority of heaven and earth, we will be like Alice in Wonderland. If we do not know which way we're going, it does not matter which way we go.

Now what should we do? The answer is simple. Adorn the civil constitution with moral truth from the ultimate authority, which is the Word of God. Wrap it with the kind of dignity you would expect from royal dignity. The church and state has the duty to appeal to the ultimate authority that will insure true liberty and real justice.

22. Easter

Once a year many Christians around the world will celebrate Easter. It is the time of the year when bunny rabbits and eggs are used as fertility symbols of this celebration. It is a religious event celebrated by various Churches professing the Christian faith.

Have you ever wondered where Christians got the name Easter? Obviously Christians use the word to describe the day that the Lord Jesus Christ was resurrected from the dead. But again I ask: how did the church arrive at the word Easter.

The word Easter was popularized by the English Monk Bede. The word Easter is believed to come from an old German root word meaning "the dawn" or the "rising of the sun." That same German word was also the name of the "spring goddess."

Through the centuries tradition passed on to each generation the folklore of that pagan German holiday and Christians have gladly received the celebration into the liturgy of the church. Socrates Scholasticus, a 4th century Christian leader concluded:

> So also the feast of Easter came to be observed in each place according to the individual peculiarities of the peoples inasmuch as none of the apostles legislated on the matter. And that the observance originated not by legislation, but as a custom the facts themselves indicate. (Socrates Scholasticus, 4th century)

The church should remember that the Scots disagreed with the Calvinistic Genevans by refusing to celebrate Christmas and Easter, because there was no warrant to do so in the Bible. The idea of a special worship service on Easter is nothing more than tradition. The New Testament never mentions any other time or occasion to worship except on the first day of the week, later called the Lord's Day, because it was the day in which the Lord rose from the dead.

The reason that Easter grew into the fantastic tradition that it is today is because the state church of the Roman Empire developed a liturgical system to accommodate the power brokers and the money machine of the church. As it is today in the majority of the church, they used visual representations to attract people and garner support.

However, God's people filled with the Spirit of God must use their rational powers to discern and understand the Word of God. The legislation given in the Word of God is that we must have 52 Easter services a year. Every Lord's Day the people that belong to Jesus Christ should gather and worship Him. Why? Not just because of tradition and not just because we're commanded to worship Him, but because we love and adore Him as our Lord and Savior.

God's grace should be seen by Christians in the fullest sense of the word. It is ridiculous to try to dissect God like you would a frog in a biology class. It is a smack in Lord's face to worship his birth on one Lord's Day and the death on another Lord's Day and His resurrection on another Lord's Day thereby separating one day from the other.

Repentance to life includes every aspect of God's saving grace from the birth of Jesus Christ to His resurrection and yes throughout all eternity. Our salvation and our worship must never be separated. As Peter learned it is never wise to argue against God. I ask the question: Who can argue against God?

I ask that question in light of the conversion of Gentile Roman Army Officer, Cornelius. Peter was called to the carpet by the Jewish religious party in Jerusalem because Peter went in and ate with a Gentile. It was no violation of the Bible for a Jew to eat with a Gentile. It was a violation of Jewish tradition.

God gave the law to the Israelites during their wilderness trials. After 16 centuries Jewish tradition had distorted what God originally intended the law to mean and accomplish.

Then Jesus Christ came and fulfilled the law. Salvation should have been easy to understand and worship was simplified, but what happened? Early in the history of the New Testament church tradition began to replace the Word of God. Now 16 centuries later salvation is grossly misunderstood and worship is as complicated as it was before the coming of Christ. Liturgy is a term used to describe the formula for public worship. If a local particular church establishes its liturgy according to unbiblical tradition, it is false worship. Unfortunately for many local churches liturgy has replaced or at least has become more important than the meaning of God's word. I do not understand why Christians cherish tradition? Tradition cannot save anyone. Tradition will not comfort you in your time of need. God alone can comfort you and save you.

Peter's meeting with Cornelius and subsequent defense before the apostles and other brethren has a great lesson for the contemporary church. (Read the whole story in Acts 10:24 – 11:18.)

It is strange to me that the good news of Cornelius' conversion did not bring rejoicing and happiness. Instead Peter was chastised, rebuked, and censured. In fact this event ultimately brought division to the church. Why did these religious people, who say they believe in God, want to argue with God? By the way, Peter was not innocent of presumptuous resistance to God's word.

God gave Peter specific instructions to "kill and eat" but good old Peter said, "Not so Lord." Even though Peter received the words directly from God, Peter resisted God's word. It may be said that Peter was simply following the regulations in the ceremonial law, but the language is such that Peter would have understood. First, Peter knew very well that God could and did repeal the ceremonial laws. Secondly, Peter knew the instructions were to offer the animals without making any distinction between the clean and the unclean animals.

Anyhow, God believes in perspicuity. When God speaks it is clear, but sinful minds are not very keen on clearness. Again God told Peter "What God has cleansed you must not call common."

The argument was over. Peter finally understood that God had destroyed the wall between Israel and the Gentiles. It was not easy, but Peter finally came to grips with God's truth, the truth that supremely surpassed the tradition of the Jews. The question that Peter never seemed to learn is that you can't argue against God. God always wins the argument.

As soon as the religious leaders in Jerusalem heard of Peter's obedience to God over the repealed ceremonial laws, they were ready to argue with Peter. The New King James Version interprets it in terms of they "contended" with him. Peter came and listened to them, but was ready to present his argument, from the facts and by the witness of six men. One of the best ways to remove misunderstanding is to stick with the facts. Deal with reality.

What were the facts? First, God spoke to Peter and to Cornelius. Second, God repealed the ceremonial laws. Third, the Holy Spirit fell upon them.

You would think that God's direct discourse and the supernatural appearance of the Holy Spirit would be sufficient to not only convince Peter, but anyone else that the Gentiles are saved by the grace of God.

But Peter did not depend on the immediate work of God and probably for a good reason; he couldn't reduplicate the event thereby leaving some question as to the validity of his claims.

If Peter's opponents were Judaizing Christians, and I expect they were, then they could not argue with the word of the Lord. But what about their precious tradition? During the Easter holiday season every professing Christian should ask the question: Who am I to think I could oppose God?

How did the church respond to Peter's facts, his interpretation, and his gracious appeal? They rejoiced in praise that the Gentiles had been granted repentance to life. Who gave them repentance? It was our Lord whose bodily resurrection must be remembered every Lord's day of the year, not just on one particular Sunday.

This text should cause Christians to rethink those things that have been handed down to them. If God has granted you repentance to life and you belong to Jesus Christ, then make Him your object of worship in your personal life, your familial life and the when you gather to worship with God's family on the Lord's Day. The only place tradition has in public worship is if it is derived from the full counsel of God!

23. Examples of Theological Ignorance

Mending the torn theological ignorance of evangelical Christianity is like the blind man telling his deaf child, "listen to me!" I wrote a book in 1996 that received limited distribution, but I do recall a pastor calling me to say that the book had caused a disturbance in the church. After he chastised me, I asked him if it was true or false. He responded, "that's not the point." Yes, truth is the point of the entire Christian life and experience. Biblical truth is necessary to restore theological integrity. Two examples of theological ignorance will suffice to illustrate the need for reformation.

Millions of professing Christians do not understand the basic Christian doctrine of the church. The cultural milieu of the western world has successfully beleaguered professing Christians into the notion that "church" is something you go to. I've heard it *ad nauseam*, "Let's go to church" or "I went to church" as if the church is a place, institution, or even worse, a building. The Holy Spirit will enable a person to be a member of the church (the body of Christ) one time in this life. The new believer (Christian) as an individual becomes part of the collective church. Then he or she and other Christians will meet collectively as a church to worship and carry out the mission and ministry of the church.

When I go into a public arena I will greet someone only to hear the response, "I'm good!" I realize that most of them do not have any serious training in biblical doctrine or theology. I realize that most of them do not understand the doctrine of the noetic effect of sin or the doctrine of original sin. Total depravity is also foreign to them and when they do stumble over a biblical text like Psalm 51:5, they dismiss it with the old, "I know what the Bible says, but... ." Many people do not stop and think before they use words. Obviously, the word "good" is merely an adjective that describes a quality of life. There are, no doubt, hundreds of definitions or nuances to the definition of the word "good." The thinking Christian will qualify the word "good" or the concept of "goodness" to the moral condition of the object of goodness. God is morally perfect, therefore He is morally good. Man's essential condition is moral imperfection, therefore he is morally bad. The Bible teaches that man is not basically good; he is basically bad. His thoughts and actions may produce good (an indefinite quality) only if the good works are mediated by Christ and according to the will of God. This is going way too long, so let me summarize.

Since the Bible indicates that all human beings are sinners and continue in sin (Rom. 3:23), they cannot possibly be "good." Like Jesus said, "No one is good [the essence of moral goodness] but One, that is, God" (Mark 10:18). Christians are declared righteous, but they are not made good. The Westminster assembly explained in these terms: "From this original corruption, whereby we are utterly indisposed, disabled, and made opposite to all good, and wholly inclined to all evil, do proceed all actual transgressions" (*Westminster Confession of Faith* 6.4). The Confession further explains: "This corruption of nature, during this life, does remain in those who are regenerated; and although it be, through Christ, pardoned, and put to death; yet the corruption of nature, and all the demonstrations of it, are truly and properly sin" (Ibid., 6.5). Suggestion: Humble yourself, trust Christ, and do good works. I think I heard a faint voice that said, "I know what the Bible says, but... ."

24. Forgiveness

Do you ever feel guilty? The word guilt means that some punishment is due for some unlawful action or behavior. People are born guilty, because they inherit the guilt of Adam. Although God created Adam a perfect man, Adam sinned and the guilt of his sin passes on to all people. "Behold, I was brought forth in iniquity, and in sin did my mother conceive me" (Psalm 51:5). You not only inherited Adam's sin nature; you also practice sin against God and against other people. "Everyone who practices sin also practices lawlessness; and sin is lawlessness" (1 John 3:4). The Bible states, "all have sinned and fall short of the glory of God" (Romans 3:23). When people sin against God, there is a broken relationship. When people sin against each other, there is a broken relationship. The only way to have the guilt removed and restore the relationship is to pay for the sin or have someone else pay the penalty for you. Your sin erects a wall between you and God. Sin severs the relationship between God and man. The only remedy for that separation is forgiveness. Is there any forgiveness? Yes, through the shed blood of the Lord Jesus Christ who paid the penalty of death for those whom God has called to Himself.

Sin causes guilt and forgiveness is the only way to relieve the guilt and heal the broken relationship. It is the guilt of sin that burns in the human heart. So, how is the guilt removed? Confession, repentance and forgiveness remove it. Martin Luther said the "forgiveness of sins through Christ is the highest article of our faith." The reason Luther said that is because of his understanding of God's holiness and man's sinful heart. You may take great comfort in the inspired words of the apostle Paul. "God has reconciled us to Himself through Jesus Christ and given us the ministry of reconciliation" (2 Corinthians 5:18).

The only way to know how to forgive is to model our forgiveness after God's forgiveness. The Bible says "be kind to one another, tenderhearted, forgiving one another, even as God in Christ forgave you" (Ephesians 4:32).

God's pattern of forgiveness in the Bible begins with confession. "If we confess our sins, He is faithful and righteous to forgive us our sins and to cleanse us from all unrighteousness" (1 John 1:9). Confession is part of forgiveness because confession is the means of verbalizing the offense. Repentance is also necessary for forgiveness. "Be on your guard! If your brother sins, rebuke him; and if he repents, forgive him"(Luke 17:3). Repentance is a change of mind and endeavor to turn to God in obedience. To put it another way, repentance is a change of attitude and direction.

We pattern our forgiveness after God by saying "I will forgive their wickedness and remember their sins no more" (Jeremiah 31;43). "As far as the east is from the west, so far has he removed our transgressions from us" (Psalm 103:12). Feelings don't determine the reality of forgiveness. What counts is objective reality, which is found in the word of God. We must judge with truth, not how we feel about truth. God doesn't forgive because he feels like it. God forgives because of his grace and mercy.

Does anyone deserve forgiveness? The Bible says, "If you O Lord, kept a record of sins, O Lord who could stand?" (Psalm 130:3). God, by His pure grace, forgives you of your multiplied sins against Him. If you believe in the forgiveness of sins you believe that you have been forgiven of the thousands upon thousands of sins that have been removed by the sacrifice of the Lord Jesus Christ.

Therefore, you must pattern your forgiveness after God's forgiveness. To forgive the other person means to remove from your mind any wrath, hatred, or desire for revenge. To forgive means to willingly, gladly, generously, and finally forget any injustice you may have experienced in your relationships with other people. Forgiveness means that the sin will never be brought up again and the relationship is restored, thus reconciliation of the two parties. God promises to forgive, but woe to the person who refuses to forgive and be reconciled.

When we practice or refuse to practice the biblical doctrine of forgiveness, it is evidence of a spiritual condition. I cannot stress mutual forgiveness enough. The doctrine is very clear. God, by His pure grace, forgives you of your multiplied sins against Him, then you must forgive others who sin against you. When you forgive, truly forgive, you are simply following the example of your Lord and give evidence of the grace of the Lord Jesus Christ present in your soul. If you are not able to forgive others who have offended you and sinned against you, then you have not received any forgiveness from God. The Lord says, "For if you forgive men their trespasses, your heavenly Father will also forgive you. But if you do not forgive men their trespasses, neither will your Father forgive your trespasses."

The result of forgiveness is reconciliation. Reconciliation is not optional among believers. Reconciliation means peace. Do you want peace with God and peace with other Christians? If the answer is yes, I urge you to remember the words of the Psalmist. "I acknowledged my sin to Thee, And my iniquity I did not hide; I said, I will confess my transgressions to the Lord; And Thou didst forgive the guilt of my sin "(Psalm 32:5).

Review the three elements necessary for forgiveness:

> God commands confession for forgiveness. Confess means you acknowledge the sin and agree with your brother that it is sin (1 John 1:9; James 5:16; Matthew 18:15).
>
> Repentance is necessary if the confession is sincere and true; "Take heed to yourselves. If your brother sins against you, rebuke him; and if he repents, forgive him" (Luke 17:3).
>
> Reconciliation is just as important as repentance. Forgiveness means that the sin will never be brought up again and the relationship is restored (Matthew 5:24; 2 Corinthians 5:18-19; Psalm 103:12).

The one word I want and I hope you want the same written on your headstone is: Forgiven.

25. God's Covenant Promises

This is for God's children who are interested in covenant theology; a serious look at God's covenant promises. And some of you are my friends. God's covenant promises are perpetual. The doctrine of the New Covenant mentioned in Jeremiah 31:31-34 simply fulfills all the previous covenant promises in the person and work of Jesus Christ, who was to come, who is and who will be. The New Covenant brings to light the fullness of God's redemptive plan through His covenant promises. The New Covenant is a triad doctrine.

The first component is that God will put His law in their minds and write the law on their hearts. Looking back at the law covenant, we find that God externalized his law on tablets of stone for the good of His people, but in the New Covenant, it is said that God "writes the law in their minds, and their hearts" (Jeremiah 31:33). Specifically the passage teaches that the Old Covenant, which was external in nature, being written on tablets of stone, will now become internally written by the Spirit on the hearts of God's people. The prophet does not mean that the only knowledge of the law of God was written on those stone tablets prior to the fulfillment of the New Covenant. Long before Jeremiah's prophesy, the Psalmist said, "Your law is within my heart" (Psalm 40:8). The apostle Paul makes it clear that the law was written on the hearts of all men (Romans 2:14-15). What Jeremiah means is that the law of God is not a loathsome law in the New Covenant. The saints of the New Covenant have a clearer understanding of God's gracious grace by the redemptive work of the Lord Jesus Christ. Under the New Covenant, the Holy Spirit causes the believer to see the acuteness of violating God's law. Then it follows that we will see the magnified beauty of Christ, who is the keeper of the law. Under the New Covenant, God's people not only want to see the magnified beauty of Christ; they want to see Christ being formed in the soul. It is the preaching of the Word and the administration of the sacraments (Baptism and Lord's Supper) that imprint the image of Christ on the heart and soul. When the Holy

Spirit writes the law on the heart, the law is then loved by God's people.

The second component of the New Covenant unites God's covenant people. "No more shall every man teach his neighbor, and every man his brother saying, "Know the Lord, for they all shall know Me, from the least of them to the greatest of them…" (Jeremiah 31:34). This aspect of the New Covenant does not militate against the duty required of external religious instruction. It does mean that Gentiles and Jews alike, individually, would have immediate access to God through the Lord Jesus Christ. Under the Old Covenant, human mediation by the priest was essential for understanding ones relationship with God. Of course, that was a mere antetype of the ultimate Mediator, the Lord Jesus Christ.

The third component of the New Covenant was the full revelation of man's greatest need, the forgiveness of sin and sins. "I will forgive their iniquity, and their sin I will remember no more" (Jeremiah 31:34). After centuries of repeated sacrifices seeking the forgiveness of sin, God promises full and final forgiveness, a promise that required the death of God's only son, the Lord Jesus Christ.

The Mediator of the New Covenant is Jesus Christ. His blood is the basis on which the blessings of this covenant comes to the covenant people of God (Hebrews 12:24). God's covenant people serve the King as effective ministers.

The efficacious work of the Holy Spirit precedes the effective work of a minister. An effective minister will herald God's message, but he does not have the authority or power to make the message accomplish its purpose. Only the efficacious work of the Holy Spirit causes the message to accomplish its purpose. The preservation and the perpetuity of the gospel are safe and secure because of the power and ability of God working through the lives of His effective ministers. Paul said God has "made us sufficient as ministers of the New Covenant."

The opponents of God's New Covenant will try to trample underfoot the gospel of Christ. Christians must grasp, believe, trust, and practice the foundation upon which he or she may build an understanding of New Covenant theology. "Not that we are sufficient of ourselves to think of anything as being from ourselves, but our sufficiency is from God" (2 Corinthians 3:5).

26. God's Mouthpiece

In the Old Testament, a watchman served in one of several capacities. Watchmen were stationed on city walls so they could alert the city if hostile action threatened the city. Watchmen were also appointed to watch over fields and vineyards during the time of harvest.

The prophets used the term "watchman" as a metaphor to describe a prophet as a spokesman for God. It was the duty of the watchman to announce to the people of God either good news or impending doom.

God commissioned the prophet Ezekiel to serve as a watchman for the house of Israel. Interestingly enough Ezekiel had already been taken captive to Babylon and apparently ministered to a group of Jewish captives by the River Chebar. You might call them the underground church of the Old Testament. Ezekiel spoke words of hope concerning the restoration of the Old Testament saints to the land of their forefathers. Ezekiel also spoke words of judgment to the Old Testament saints in exile. His warning was, "turn to the Lord, because God delighted in those who turn from sin."

Ezekiel's words are as fresh as this morning's newspaper and we need to hear afresh the Word of God delivered from the mouthpiece of God. The mouthpiece of God must announce to the people of God the law and the gospel for the benefit of their own spiritual nurture and growth. The evangelical church is at a point of crisis. All too often the shepherds are slumbering and not watching for the wolves as they subtly separate the flock by their charm and false doctrine.

The necessity imposed on ministers to proclaim the whole counsel of God is not to be taken lightly by the pastor or the congregation. If the preacher neglects to preach the whole counsel of God, then the preacher has neglected to warn the congregation of God's impending judgment. If the preacher neglects God's warning, the congregation will perish.

> I have made you a watchman for the house of Israel; therefore you shall hear a word from My mouth and warn them for Me.

> When I say to the wicked, "O wicked man, you shall surely die! and you do not speak to warn the wicked from his way, that wicked man shall die in his iniquity; but his blood I will require at your hand (Ezekiel 33:7-8).

If the preacher neglects God's mandate, the minister himself will be dealt with as the author of that sinner's destruction. The responsibility placed on the watchman is a profound obligation.

I cannot stress enough the emphasis that God places on the preaching of the word. The examples from Scripture are not very pleasing to the ear.

> If any man is preaching to you a gospel contrary to that which you received, let him be accursed. (Galatians 1:9)

> Some to be sure, are preaching Christ even from envy and strife, but some also from good will. (Philippians 1:15)

> Furthermore, when I came to Troas to preach Christ's gospel, and a door was opened to me by the Lord, I had no rest in my spirit, because I did not find Titus my brother; but taking my leave of them, I departed for Macedonia. Now thanks be to God who always leads us in triumph in Christ, and through us diffuses the fragrance of His knowledge in every place. For we are to God the fragrance of Christ among those who are being saved and among those who are perishing. To the one we are the aroma of death leading to death, and to the other the aroma of life leading to life. And who is sufficient for these things? For we are not, as so many, peddling the word of God; but as of sincerity, but as from God, we speak in the sight of God in Christ. (2 Corinthians 2:12-17)

Paul's scathing analysis of false preachers ought to bring fear to the soul of any man preparing to preach a sermon. Too much preaching today is a fake; false preachers are "peddling" the Word of God. Preaching the Word of God has a fragrance. To some people it smells bad and to others it smells good. Sound preaching from the

Word of God is a good aroma to God but is a stench to the nostrils of those who are in an unfavorable relation with God.

How must God's mouthpiece speak to God's people? "I have made you a watchman for the house of Israel; therefore you shall hear a word from My mouth and warn them for Me" (Ezekiel 33:11). God's mouthpiece, Ezekiel, received his words directly from God by inspiration. Today God's mouthpiece, the preacher, must consult the Word of God that was given by inspiration to know how to speak God's words. The only way a preacher can preach sound doctrine is to consult the Word of God. Unfortunately there are many preachers today who consult the enticing words of man's wisdom to preach the word of God. Preaching and teaching the Word of God must not be intermingled with "persuasive words of human wisdom" so says the Apostle Paul and he goes on to say that preaching must be of the Spirit and of power, that your faith should not be in the wisdom of men but in the power of God.

The pastors that are called to labor in the ministry of the Word are to preach sound doctrine. Paul explained this doctrine to Timothy. "Hold fast the pattern of sound words which you have heard from me…" (2 Timothy 1:13).

The pew has the duty to hear the preacher. How must God's mouthpiece, the preacher, be heard by God's people, the pew? "Whoever hears the sound of the trumpet and does not take warning, if the sword comes and takes him away his blood shall be on his own head. He heard the sound of the trumpet, but did not take warning" (Ezekiel 33:4-5).

The trumpet allegorically represents the Word of God. The law and the gospel of God's grace constitute the Word of God. The law is needed to show man his sin and the gospel is needed to save man from his sin.

The function of the Hebrew verb *shama* translated "he heard" may be either a completed action or an instantaneous action. The context makes me believe that the sound was instantaneously impressive and even startling.

The *Westminster Larger Catechism* question number 160 is thought provoking. The question, "What is required of those that hear the Word preached?" may be summarized under the these points:

1. They must attend upon the preaching with diligence.
2. They must prepare for the preaching of the Word of God.
3. They must attend the preaching prayerfully.
4. They must examine what they hear by the Scriptures.
5. They must receive the truth with faith, love, meekness and readiness of mind.
6. They must meditate and confer upon the preaching.
7. They must hide the preaching in their hearts.
8. They must bring forth the fruit of the preaching in their lives.

The preacher is appointed by God to watch over the souls committed to his charge. If he faithfully and fearfully fulfills his responsibility as a mouthpiece for God, then God's people are obligated to receive and take pleasure in the doctrine of the true and living God. God's watchmen must be prepared to be God's mouthpiece. God's mouthpiece must have a passion for the Word of God and those who hear from God must have a passion to be reformed by the Word of God. Do you have that passion?

The preaching of the Word of God may convict you of sin in your life and that is good. However, the preaching of the Word of God will build you up and strengthen you to serve God.

27. God's People are Praying People

God refers to Israel in the Old Testament as "My people" (Exodus 3:10; Jeremiah 7:12; et al.) and in the New Testament God's people are the church. People are bi-dimensional; they have physical properties and spiritual properties. The spiritual dimension has two categories: The saved (Christian believers) and the unsaved (atheists). (Jesus explains the difference between the Christian and the atheist in John 8:42-47.) Atheists are not able to pray to God. The *Westminster Larger Catechism* explains why.

> The sinfulness of man, and his distance from God by reason thereof, being so great, as that we can have no access into his presence without a mediator; and there being none in heaven or earth appointed to, or fit for, that glorious work but Christ alone, we are to pray in no other name but his only. (*Westminster Larger Catechism*, 181)

Jesus Christ is the only true Mediator. However, there are many fake mediators, for example:

> Jesus Christ that saves everyone
> Jesus Christ of the emerging church movement
> Jesus Christ of the Jehovah's Witness
> Jesus Christ of the postmodern church
> Jesus Christ that was not physically resurrected
> Jesus Christ the antinomian
> Jesus Christ of the new age movement
> Jesus Christ who believes justification by works
> Jesus Christ who believes in continuing revelation
> Jesus Christ the Son of the living God, the sinless God-man, the second person of the trinity, defined by the whole counsel of God without contradiction.

Obviously one must be careful not to bend the knee in prayer, if the prayer is offered in the name of a fake Jesus. The Bible teaches that all men must pray, but Scripture teaches that prayers from unbelievers are unacceptable (Psalm 66:18, Proverbs 28:9). What is the resolution? Unbelievers must be converted before God will find their prayers acceptable, even though He requires all men to pray. Likewise God requires all men to keep his law, but in their unconverted state they cannot obey. The prayers of unconverted men will add to the other sins they commit by omission or commission. What should they do? Seek the Lord while He may be found and believe on the Lord Jesus Christ. Then, the prayer of the converted sinner will have the Mediator, the Lord Jesus Christ, so the prayer will be acceptable to God.

Misinterpreting Scripture often leads professing Christians to pray contrary to the teaching of Scripture. For instance, taking a text of Scripture out of context can have undesirable effects.

I'll give one example of how evangelicals confuse political theory with church doctrine. Professing Christians often quote the Bible with great passion:

> [I]f My people who are called by My name will humble themselves, and pray and seek My face, and turn from their wicked ways, then I will hear from heaven, and will forgive their sin and heal their land. (2 Chronicles 7:14)

Ripped out of the context of Solomon's completion of building the temple in Jerusalem, his dedication of it, and the worship associated with it, professing Christians apply this verse to the United States (although they are very un-united at this kairotic juncture in history). This verse comes out of God's appearance to Solomon. God said, "My people (the church) who are called by My name." Then in verse 15 God said, "I have chosen and sanctified this house, that my name may be there forever." Then in verse 18 God said, "I will establish the throne of your kingdom." NONE OF THIS REFERS TO THE UNITED STATES AS A NATION. "My people" the church should humble themselves and pray. The church ought to pray for the state. Forgiveness is another doctrine very often ignored by professing Christians…And he will never grant healing to the United States, but

God will heal His church because of the Lord Jesus Christ, by the power of the Holy Spirit.

28. Hell Is Real

Reality holds my attention exceedingly greater than the religious gibberish in the modern/postmodern professing church. Sermons and lectures are useless unless their content is real, truthful and deliberately focused on a doctrine from the Word of God. I particularly like to study the reality of spiritual and metaphysical dimensions. Not well accepted in this postmodern age are discussions about the metaphysical realities. Obviously people do not like to think about what happens when the physical body dies. However, that is metaphysical. In reality, the Bible is an inspired record of metaphysical topics.

Heaven is metaphysical; hell is metaphysical. Of course, heaven is widely accepted and from my experience most people believe that when a person dies, he or she goes to heaven. I can't remember hearing a sermon on eternal punishment in the past 25 years. Professing Christians are becoming less and less inclined to believe the biblical truth that hell refers to eternal punishment of unbelievers and professing believers who are merely professors only.

The tragedy is the watchmen are not blowing the trumpets and warning the people (Ezekiel 33:1-10). "Some people are in churches which allow their members to go to hell because they do not preach the gospel they profess. Other religious groups can guarantee hell because they do preach the false gospel they profess. Others have no gospel at all; an absolutely sure way to damnation" (*Repent or Perish*, Dr. John Gerstner, p. 192).

Jonathan Edwards was not afraid to preach on the awful doctrine of hell. He preached over 40 sermons on the subject and mentioned hell 60 times in his *Miscellanies*. Dr. John Gerstner was a noted authority on the life and doctrine of Jonathan Edwards. Dr. Gerstner defined hell using the expressions found in Edward's sermons.

> Hell is a spiritual and material furnace of fire, where its victims are exquisitely tortured, in their minds and in their bodies eternally, according to their various capacities, by God,

the devils, and damned humans, including themselves, in their memories and consciences, as well as in their raging, unsatisfied lusts, from which place of death God's saving grace, mercy, and pity are gone forever – never for a moment to return" (*Rational Biblical Theology of Jonathan Edwards*, vol. 3, p. 503).

Professing evangelical theologians in recent church history have denied the doctrine of hell. John Stott, Philip Hughes, and Edward Fudge threatened to put out the fires of hell with their annihilationism. They should read and study the Bible carefully using the fundamental principles of Reformed hermeneutics. It has been said that hades does not refer to hell. They need to read Luke 16:23 carefully. Hades is the place of torment and is commonly referred to as hell.

Hell is not a very popular subject. People generally don't like to think about Hell, yet Jesus spoke of Hell and eternal damnation as much as He spoke of Heaven and its glorious nature. The misery of Hell may be described as the wrath of God poured out on children of Satan with unmitigated punishment. Human beings fit into one of two categories: children of God or children of Satan. Children of God will spend eternity in the new heavens and new earth enjoying a favorable relation with God. Children of Satan will spend eternity in hell tortured by the wrath of God.

The Book of Revelation describes hell as the "wrath of God which is poured out, full strength, into the cup of His indignation." Hell is the place where the ungodly "shall be tormented with fire and brimstone in the presence of the holy angels and in the presence of the Lamb. And the smoke of their torment ascends forever and ever; and they have no rest day or night…" (Revelation 14:10-11).

The Bible is clear; the "wrath of God is poured out in full strength." God's wrath is poured out without mixture. In hell there is no grace, there is no moderation, and there is no end to God's wrath. The Bible paints a picture of God's full fury and fierceness in that awful place.

Paul wrote the Thessalonian Church and warned that Jesus Christ will be revealed "in flaming fire taking vengeance on those who do not know God and on those who do not obey the gospel of the Lord Jesus Christ." These shall be punished with everlasting destruction from the presence of the Lord and from the glory of His power (2 Thessalonians 1:7). Scripture describes hell as a bottomless pit (Revelation 9:1) and the "blackness of darkness (Jude 13). Hell is compared to a lake of fire and a great furnace of fire. The agony of the flame is relentless and the pain will never to be diminished. The metaphors from Scripture are mere glimpses of the great torment. The miseries of both body and soul will never cease by the demonstration of God's justice and His power applied according to his justice.

Hell is real, but so is God's grace. Trust Jesus Christ for God's saving grace to save the soul from an eternal hell. The Holy Spirit opens the heart to enable the sinner to believe. The power of the Holy Spirit renews the mind so that the truth of the Word of God can be believed. The Holy Spirit of God changes the will so that the truth of the Word of God can be acted upon. After God changes the heart, the converted sinner must then engage tirelessly in the noble work of inquiring into God's word to discover God's promise to save His children.

There are many Bible scholars who deny the reality of hell, but their denial does not remove the reality. What a sockdolager!

29. Is the Word of God Enough?

Perspective. I recently finished reading the life and ministry of Martin Luther by Eric Metaxas. His prose was not typical historical/theological genre. He did not spend time explaining Scripture from Luther's perspective; Metaxes left that to Luther. Then I started reading Colin Brown's Philosophy and the Christian Faith. I didn't get very far and realized, "I already know this" so why am I reading it? He is a scholar, but has ordination credentials with a liberal denomination; he also teaches at a seminary that does not boldly and manifestly embrace the infallibility of the Word of God. The dispute over the infallibility of Scripture has been on-going for over 50 years. I've ditched Brown and will find a book that will exercise my cognitive ability.

The title of this article derived from my musing of the collective body of Christians and realizing that so many professing Christians individually and entire denominations are not satisfied with the Word of God. Without explicitly saying it they imply the Word of God is not enough. Luther believed the Word of God was enough. Colin Brown does not believe the Word of God is enough. Even if they do believe the Bible is sufficient for faith and life, they believe there are many and various interpretations. However, there are a few who believe their interpretation is the only correct and orthodox interpretation. Everybody else will go to hell.

It is popular to argue that the church will prosper if more faith healers would get busy in ministry. To put it another way more miracles are needed today. I've only seen one miracle over the past 71 years. It happened about 30 years ago. I was in Anderson's hospital in Meridian, MS for some tests. I'm the only one aware that a miracle had occurred. It was simple. One day I had no interest in God or any spiritual reality and certainly had no belief that the Bible was any more important than any other book. The next day I believed God was real and eternal, and most importantly I believed the Bible was absolutely true. I've seen many experience that same miracle. Believing the Bible is the Word of God and believing the numerous miracles recorded in the Word of God is the great need in the church today. It was also needed 500 years ago. In one of Martin Luther's letters he wrote, "A simple layman armed with Scripture is to be believed above a pope or a council without it" (p. 176).

Unbelievers will not be persuaded the Bible is the Word of God. However, believers are persuaded by the power of God's Spirit that the Bible is the Word of God. The Holy Spirit reveals the truth and reality in the Word of God. The child of God will not grow weary of hearing God's Word. He or she would never say, "God's Word is redundant." The child of God has no reason to say, "the Word of God is not enough." However, the authority of God's Word is self-evident.

> God's Word is supernatural in its content.
> God's Word is sufficient in its teaching.
> God's Word reflects the majesty and aseity of God.
> God's Word is not contradictory in any of its parts.
> God's Word reveals the only way of man's salvation.
> God's Word discovers the meaning of faith and life.
> God's Word reflects the perfection of all its parts.

The evidence for belief that the Word of God is true will be reflected in our actions. If Christians actually believe that God is the almighty creator, that He upholds and sustains what He creates, and that God provides for His creation, then God's people should desire His Word personally and passionately.

For unbelievers, the Word of God is an intolerable set of rules that must be destroyed and replaced with the lies of Satan, which will lead one to death and eternal punishment. Even so, unbelievers should be encouraged to read it because from it they may see their sin and need for a Savior. The Word of God reveals the way of salvation.

The Word of God is for God's people, for it speaks to them and they gladly believe it. For God's people His Word is a treasure - a treasure that will lead one to life and eternal praises to the Lord God Almighty. Is the Word of God Enough?

30. True Gospel: Forensic Justification

I listen to sermons online, rarely, and yesterday was a rare occasion. I did not have any connection or knowledge of the church or preacher. The denomination professes to be evangelical and "Bible-believing." It is rare for me to listen to a superficial sermon online, but I listened to this particular sermon on the doctrine of the resurrection while I was working on my commentary of the book of Ephesians. Near the end of the sermon the preacher made this statement: "I'm glad the resurrection of Jesus Christ made me righteous." A sockdolager I thought, so I listened to the video again and sure enough he said "made me righteous." I would expect to hear that doctrine from a Roman Catholic, but not from an evangelical preacher. I've studied, lectured, taught, preached and written on the doctrine of justification, but to my chagrin I've never written a brief paper on the doctrine. Here is my commentary of the doctrine of "justification by faith alone."

What is justification?

> Answer from the *Westminster Confession of Faith*: "Those whom God effectually calls, He also freely justifies; not by infusing righteousness into them, but by pardoning their sins, and by accounting and accepting their persons as righteous; not for anything produced in them, or done by them, but for Christ's sake alone; nor by imputing faith itself, the act of believing, or any other evangelical obedience to them, as their righteousness; but by imputing the obedience and satisfaction of Christ unto them, they receiving and resting on Him and His righteousness by faith; which faith they have not of themselves, it is the gift of God."

Martin Luther believed that the doctrine of justification was the article by which the church stands or falls. The salvation of the soul is the central aspect of the doctrine of justification. Another 17th century theologian said, "By other Christians, it is termed the characteristic and basis of Christianity – not without reason – the principle rampart of the Christian religion" (*Institutes of Elenctic Theology*, Francis Turretin, vol. 2, p. 633). The Bible is not ambiguous. "And he [Abram] believed in the LORD, and He accounted it to him for righteousness." The New Testament clarifies the Old Testament: "Therefore, having been justified by faith, we have peace with God through our Lord Jesus Christ, through whom also we have access by faith into this grace in which we stand, and rejoice in hope of the glory of God" (Romans 5:1-2).

The word "justification" used in relation to the doctrine of salvation in Scripture is always used in a forensic (legal) sense. It is a divine act whereby, God declares the children of God, who are sinners and deserve condemnation, to be acceptable in His sight. The Bible uses forensic (legal) language in the explanation of our standing before God. For instance, "Who shall bring a charge against God's elect? It is God who justifies" (Romans 8:33). Obviously justification is opposed to condemnation. Therefore, we find again judicial language used to describe and explain this important doctrine.

The doctrine of justification does not infuse the righteousness of Christ into the believer, but the righteousness of Christ is imputed (credited, accounted) to the sinner. The following chart, derived from the teaching of Dr. John Gerstner, explains the various views of justification. He used the following formula in his seminary classes.

Reformed Theology--------Faith = Justification + Works

Antinomianism--------------Faith = Justification – Works

Liberalism-------------------Works = Justification – Faith

Romanism-------------------Faith + Works = Justification

The Bible teaches that the alone instrument of justification is faith (See Romans 3:28; 5:1). Nothing can be added to your believing in Christ or as *Westminster* explains, "receiving and resting on Christ and his righteousness" is all a person can do for the salvation of his or her soul. Believing that Jesus Christ is the son of God and believing that Jesus Christ is a ticket to heaven is not the same as "receiving and resting" on Christ. It has been said that the only thing a man can participate in salvation is to appropriate his faith. The faith does not actually belong to the sinner, because God gives the sinner the ability to believe. It is with confidence that Christians believe that the righteousness of Christ is sufficient to remove God's eternal wrath against the sinner.

The Bible is also anti-antinomianism (antinomianism means that no good works should follow faith). It is soundly biblical to say, "Faith...is...not alone in the person justified." This is precisely the meaning of James 2:17: "Thus also faith by itself, if it does not have works, is dead." Faith will always be accompanied by other saving graces. There must be evidence to accompany the faith. It is insensitive and contrary to common sense to believe that something exists that does not exist. Therefore, works will follow faith. Dr. Francis Beattie's commentary on this part of the confession explains how "good works are the assured fruits of justifying faith and growth in grace certainly appears in this state of grace."

The only way a sinner can be "declared" in a favorable relation with God is by the satisfaction of God's justice. Too often it is said the sinner's justification is free. It should be correctly stated that justification is a free gift. However, the gift required payment and Christ freely gave Himself for that payment. The gift is free, or to put it another way, the grace is free to the recipient, but it was not free to the divine Son of God. It was Christ and his obedience and death that paid the debt thus satisfying God's justice.

The doctrine of justification must be distinguished from the doctrine of regeneration (the new heart, born again). The doctrine of regeneration changes the condition of the soul, but regeneration does not remove the guilt of Adam's sin. Although the Holy Spirit changes the heart so that the soul dead in sin is renewed, the guilt that brings with it condemnation, must be removed by the doctrine of justification.

Christians must be careful with this doctrine that has been grossly misinterpreted throughout the centuries. False teachers believe that justification was eternal and therefore the sacrifice of Christ was not necessary. This and other errors are avoided by this precise articulation from the *Westminster Confession of Faith*. God certainly ordained that Christ would die and therefore, Christ is the ground of the sinner's justification. However, the instrument of justification is faith. Furthermore, it is faith alone with nothing added.

Francis Turretin, an evangelical 17th century theologian, wrote, "it is not controverted whether faith justifies – for Scripture so clearly asserts this that no one dares to deny it. Rather we inquire regarding the manner in which it justifies..." (*Institutes of Elenctic Theology*, vol. 2, p. 669). The Bible leaves no doubt that the Holy Spirit applies the work of Christ so that the sinner finds relief from the guilt of sin.

The doctrine of justification is described by the *Westminster Shorter Catechism* as an "act" of God. Although justification is more kairotic (point of time) than chronological (sequence of time), justification does have a lasting effect. In fact, if a sinner is justified, the result is eternal. Christians are not justified one day and unjustified the next day.

> Justification is a permanent condition of the sinner to whom the Holy Spirit applies it, but the sinner remains a sinner until he comes to a state of glory. However, justified sinners will always "confess their sins, beg pardon, and renew their faith and repentance." Confession of sin may bring humility and shame, but it is necessary for repentance. (Doctrine of Sound Words, by Martin Murphy, pg. 76)

Dispensational theology divides the salvation of men into several different categories according to God's plan for salvation for that particular time in history. The different dispensations are: Innocence; Conscience; Human Government; Promise; Law; Grace; and Kingdom. Each of the dispensations includes a new revelation from God. The *Scofield Reference Bible* explains that a dispensation is a "mode of testing" (Genesis 12, notes). In each dispensation man fails the test thus leaving God no choice but to find another way to save the people. One comment from the *Scofield Reference Bible* will suffice to prove the point: "The Dispensation of Promise [the covenant God made with Abraham, Genesis 12-17] ended when Israel rashly accepted the law [Exodus 19]" (Genesis 12, notes). The danger of Dispensationalism's divisiology is that it results in three classes of people: Israel, the descendants of Abraham; the Gentiles, the unsaved;

and the church, the Christians. This view of the Bible dangerously divides the way of salvation by making radical distinctions in the Old Testament and the New Testament way of salvation.

Covenant theology, contrary to Dispensational theology, is careful to point out that God's way of salvation is no different in the Old Testament than it is in the New Testament. For Abraham "believed in the Lord and he [the Lord] counted it to him for righteousness" (Genesis 15:6). Paul brings unity to this doctrine: "those who are of faith are blessed with Abraham, the believer" (Galatians 3:9).

Justification is an act of God so that God declares the believer righteous. God judges the believer to be innocent based on the imputed righteousness of Christ. The Roman Catholic Church claimed it was *Justitia alienum*, an alien righteousness. The Protestant view of justification teaches that Christ "declares" one righteous. *Justitia alienum* is the charge of the Roman Catholic Church against the Reformers. Rome called the Reformers view of justification by faith alone "alien" because under analysis the professing believer was not "made" righteous. According to Rome the righteousness professed by the Protestant was alien to the believer. Forensic justification is the Protestant position that justification is a legal declaration of God. Man is formally and judicially reckoned to be righteous based on the righteousness of Christ, received by faith alone. Short summary of true and false doctrine:

True gospel: God "declares" the sinner righteous
False gospel: God "makes" the sinner righteous

31. Make the Church Great Again

The United States is at war. Actually, they are not very united. The battlefields are raging with issues such as abortion, women's rights, gay rights, racial discrimination, education, economics and list goes on and on. Some people buy into the sophisticated worldview known as globalism. Others prefer traditional nationalism as a political and cultural worldview. The differences are so vast and so numerous that a global library could not contain them. Donald Trump came up with a slogan: "Make America Great, Again!"

The dilemma for the Christian church is similar to the battles being fought in the United States with a few additional problems. The church is polarized. Theological ignorance abounds. Utilitarianism is the trend. Ecclesiastical intrigue is common as fried chicken. God's law is horribly misinterpreted. Moralism has replaced justification by faith alone. For those who know me, I offer a satirical slogan: "Make the Church Great, Again!" I call it satire because that slogan is the biggest joke of the century. The church always has been great and always will be great. Nations rise and fall, but the church is eternally God's people.

James H. Thornwell, a pastor and theologian during the 19th century expressed serious concern over pragmatism and secularism associated with the church in a letter to Dr. R. J. Breckinridge, July 24, 1846:

> I am seriously afraid that the foolish liberality of the age will speedily plunge us into the same disasters from which we have just escaped. Our whole system of operations gives an undue influence to money. Where money is the great want, numbers must be sought; and where ambition for numbers prevails, doctrinal purity must be sacrificed. The root of the evil is the secular spirit of our ecclesiastical institutions. What we want is a spiritual body; a Church whose power lies in the truth, and presence of the Holy Ghost. To unsecularize the Church

should be the unceasing aim of all who are anxious that the ways of Zion should flourish.

The word church has become a byword for religious activity.

> The definition of the word "church" is not complicated, but it has several different aspects that must be considered. The word church in the Bible has nothing to do with a building. When Christians call a building the church, they either do not know the biblical meaning of the word church or they are just using the word "church" because that is what it means according to traditional language. The word church (or churches) is used in the English Bible 109 times (NASB). None of the 109 references refers to the church as a building, other than 3 references of the church meeting in a home. The Greek word *ekklesia* is translated in the English Bible as church. It refers to a local congregation of professing Christians or the total of all God's people. (*Doctrine of Sound Words*, p. 282)

The aggregate of all local congregations and every individual Christian constitute the church, the people of God, the body of Jesus Christ. Understanding the fundamental doctrine of the church will bring peace and joy to the soul.

32. Thanksgiving

Psalm 104 shows the scope of God's creative power in the works of His creation so that God demonstrates his governing hand over creation. God creates, preserves and governs all things. To understand thanksgiving one must understand God's providence. The word providence comes from two Latin words *pro* and *videre* meaning to see before hand. God is not merely a spectator, passively knowing in advance, what will happen through his foreknowledge. He knows in advance because he plans in advance. The *Westminster Shorter Catechism* explains the doctrine of providence. "God's works of providence are, His most holy, wise, and powerful preserving and governing all His creatures, and all their actions.

The *aseity* of God is rarely mentioned these days. *Aseity* refers to God's self-existence. He does not need any outside source to maintain His independent being contrary to all created dependent beings. Humans need air, water, food, and other essentials to sustain them. This is the doctrine of sustenance. The universe and everything within it is dependent on the being and power of God to sustain it. Only God has ultimate power because "in Him we live and move and have our being" (Acts 17:28). The universe was not created and left like a clock ticking away to a point of expiration. God sustains not only human life, He sustains everything in the universe to perfection. Not one molecule, not one atom, is out of place. What God creates he sustains through the work of His sustenance. God's people should not dismiss sustenance as one of those abstract doctrines that doesn't touch their lives. Sustenance is directly related to Christians through God's provision.

God not only creates and sustains, He provides for His creation. The doctrine of God's provision is a dimension that is closely associated with sustenance. God foresees all things because God has foreordained all things and therefore God responds by providing for his creation. He prepares a future and then meets all the needs of His creation. The ultimate provision is the substitutionary atonement made by Christ to satisfy the wrath of God.

The government of God is another dimension of the doctrine of providence. The government of God reflects the authority and power of God. God is the supreme Governor who rules the world, because He has the absolute authority and power to govern. God's absolute authority gives Him the right to govern all that he creates. God's power gives Him the ability to govern all that he creates. His government is the directing and disposing of all things that come to pass. There is no sphere of the created world in which God is not involved. The Bible teaches that God's rule is sovereign. "The Lord has established His throne in heaven, and His kingdom rules over all" (Psalm 103:19). The Bible also teaches that God rules righteously. "The God of Israel said...He who rules over men must be just, ruling in the fear of God" (2 Samuel 23:3). Justice and sovereignty are inalienable marks of God's providence.

The doctrine of concurrence is most important to the doctrine of God's providence. This doctrine teaches that God's plan is brought to pass by His sovereign hand through human means. This means that "it pleases God to use means outside Himself, second causes, to accomplish many things." The necessary, free, and contingent second causes concur with the eternal decrees of God in such a way that all things work out for the glory of God. Joseph's brothers sold him into slavery. They intended it for evil, but God intended it for good. The doctrine of God's providence is in the proximate world with all its evil, yet the doctrine of concurrence assures Christians that God's way has ultimate consequences.

Christians abuse God's providential care several different ways. First, they ignore God's character and expect an immediate communication by the Holy Spirit. Christians abuse God's providential care by complaining, impatience, and despair. The blessing of God's providence is sufficient to meet all your needs, so you can offer praises to Him.

Christians must seek the revealed will of God and rejoice that His providential care works out necessarily, freely, and contingently according to his sustenance, provision, and government concurrently for our good and for His glory.

There was a time in this country when thanksgiving was recognized as a legitimate aspect of life. Even the holiday we call Thanksgiving reminded people and especially Christians that all of our worldly goods were a result of God's gracious hand. Today Thanksgiving is merely a long holiday weekend that marks the beginning of Christmas shopping. There are more sales advertisements in the Thanksgiving day newspaper than any two Sunday newspapers put together. We have more goods and products being consumed today than ever before. We have more to be thankful for, in the way of material wealth, than ever before. Yet, there is less interest in thankfulness than ever before. Make this Thanksgiving holiday a truly thankful time more than ever before.

Please share this Thanksgiving message with your family and friends. Rejoice always, pray without ceasing, in everything give thanks; for this is the will of God in Jesus Christ for you" (1 Thessalonians 5:16-17).

33. The Soul of Man

I admit that most of my adult time on earth has been spent in study, contemplation, inquiry, research, and musing about life. The philosophy of life has three immediate questions that fascinate the rational mind, especially mine.

1. Where did I come from?
2. Why am I here?
3. Where am I going?

Simple questions, but rarely deliberated with any serious meditation. If you ask all three questions, secure three answers, and do that in sequence at least seven times, you will begin to lose contact with physical reality. Human beings have a short experience with physical reality, maybe eighty years at the most. I've tried to understand physical reality, or what we call life, but I don't understand to my satisfaction. In 1990 I became acquainted with two terms that has occupied my search for understanding physical reality. The term "culture wars" introduced me to the world of ungodly Individualism. I eventually wrote a book on the subject (which very few people have read), but it revealed my interest in physical reality. The term "Postmodernity" became my pet peeve (actually pesky peeve) because of its ungodly influence over the academy would devolve to the next generation, the demise of intelligent communication. It fascinates me beyond intelligence, because it denies RATIONAL intelligent discourse. So much for all the energy I put into the inquiry of my contact with physical reality. This brief quote from a 20th century philosopher will probably resonate with most anyone reading this blog. "It is surely not so bad to die, providing one has really lived before he dies. The tragedy is not that all die, but that so many fail to really live" (David Elton Trueblood).

However, the three questions I presented, if answered with any serious rational inquiry, will take you into metaphysical reality. Metaphysical, apart from all the philosophical technicalities and their derived applications, simply refers to something beyond the physical. For instance, the body is physical. The soul is metaphysical. The brain is physical, the mind is metaphysical. Of course, many people do not believe there is a metaphysical reality. They believe in "nothing" whatever that is. At this point in my life I'm losing interest in cultural wars and the postmodern concept. I've written books for the next generation as a warning and for encouragement.

Question 32.1 When the body dies, what happens to the soul?

Answer: The bodies of men, after death, return to dust, and see corruption: but their souls, which neither die nor sleep, having an immortal subsistence, immediately return to God who gave them: the souls of the righteous, being then made perfect in holiness, are received into the highest heavens, where they behold the face of God, in light and glory, waiting for the full redemption of their bodies. And the souls of the wicked are cast into hell, where they remain in torments and utter darkness, reserved to the judgment of the great day. Beside these two places, for souls separated from their bodies, the Scripture acknowledges none.

Commentary: Westminster asserts the biblical doctrine of life beyond the grave. They distinguish between the body and the soul. Every human being (person) consists of a body and soul. The body is material and physical. The soul is spiritual and metaphysical. The writer of Hebrews says, "It is appointed for men to die once" (Hebrews 9:27). This biblical reference is to the death of the body. The book of Romans says, "Through one man sin entered the world, and death through sin" (Romans 5:12). This is a reference to the spiritual death of the soul in the sense that the soul is separated from the good favor and relationship with God.

Although the body decays and ceases to function, the soul is sustained by an "immortal subsistence." Some opponents to the orthodox doctrine teach "soul sleep" and others teach "annihilation" of the soul. The soul sleep advocates maintain

> that the soul is in a state of insensibility from the death of the body until the final judgment and resurrection. The annihilation theory is more heretical by teaching that the soul of unbelievers ceases to exist. Both errors are condemned by the words of the Lord Jesus Christ recorded by inspiration in the gospel of Matthew [Matthew 10:28]. (*Doctrine of Sound Words*, page 199)

If the Lord enables me to continue writing, I plan to write a book about the soul of man. A piece of wisdom from John Calvin's Institutes.

> It is of course true that while men are tied to earth more than they should be they grow dull; indeed, because they have been estranged from the Father of Lights [James 1:17], they become blinded by darkness, so that they do not think they will survive death...for the body is not affected by the fear of spiritual punishment... .(*Institutes of the Christian Religion*, 1.15.2)

A piece of wisdom from God: "For what profit is it to a man if he gains the whole world, and loses his own soul? Or what will a man give in exchange for his soul" (Matthew 16:26)?

I found the answer to the question "Where did I come from?" The Bible teaches and I believe that God created me. I'm still seeking an answer to question "Why am I here?" I can't definitively answer that question, because I'm still here. Of course, I'm here to enjoy and worship my Creator, but there are many responsibilities depending on the time left and the intervening historical contingencies. The final question has a specific and definite answer in the Bible. However, I've never met a rational contemporary human being that has been where I am going. Since I've never been there and no one can go for me, I'll trust the one who has given me life, past, present and a promise for eternal life. Jesus Christ.

34. Where Is My Eternal Home?

In the Christian's eternal home no one goes to church but everyone is in worship. Eternal life is joy unspeakable. Life is not mere existence, because the wicked will exist forever, but under the hand of God's divine justice. "And many of those who sleep in the dust of the earth shall awake, some to everlasting life, some to shame and everlasting contempt" (Daniel 12:2). There is an eternal life for the believer and everlasting life for the unbeliever. Eternal life for the believer is difficult to contemplate with our sinful minds. Jonathan Edwards explains eternal life for the believer with graphic language.

> They shall eat and drink abundantly and swim in the ocean of love, and be eternally swallowed up on the infinitely bright, and infinitely mild and sweet beams of divine love" (*Works of Jonathan Edwards*, volume 2, page 29).

On the contrary, to exist under the mighty wrath of God and endure the everlasting punishment is for the unbeliever. The Word of God describes it as everlasting contempt (Daniel 12:2). Those who belong to Jesus Christ not only have life, they have a blessed eternal life of joy and peace.

Daniel's prophecy is an awesome truth found throughout Scripture, but there is another passage of Scripture that should cause everyone to think about eternity. "Many are called but few are chosen" (Matthew 22:14). Such a profound inspired statement should cause every person to ask the question, "Am I of that number." If we seriously ask that question and answer it honestly, it will help us understand the difference and desire for eternal life in heaven or everlasting life in hell. The glorious nature and character of heaven is inexpressible because everything in this secular life is merely a shadow, type or figure of the full expression of God's redemptive plan. In the heavenly home Christians will know God perfectly thus they can love Him perfectly, not out of mere desire, but out of utter delight in His being. Think about what it will be like to be perfect and live in a perfect environment. Perfection means no sickness, no weariness, and no need to stop and rest or take a nap. Perfection means using the human mind to the fullest degree. It has been said that even a genius employs less than ten percent of his brain. In our eternal home our minds, not our brains, will function at a hundred percent level. People talk of 20/20 vision. The book of Revelation describes the splendor of the beautiful colors in our perfected state. The glorified child of God will experience perfection of all the senses.

Have you ever experienced loneliness? In our eternal home the sin that separates us in this secular life will be removed so that we will have perfect unending communion and fellowship with one another. Think of every mystery you've ever pondered and every passage of Scripture that never was fully understandable. In our eternal home all of it will be revealed to perfection. Every Christian should desire everlasting life. "The gift of God is eternal life through Jesus Christ, our Lord" (Romans 6:23). The eternal home is not free. The Lord Jesus Christ paid a heavy price, so that the eternal home could be called "a gift" for those saved by the grace of God.

35. Worship According to God's Standard

The modern church should learn from the 16th century Reformers that "men are experts at inventing idols." They studied the Word of God and concluded that "God...cannot endure new modes of worship to be devised...All kinds of worship invented by men...are accursed and detestable." Like the 16th century Reformers,

> We must hold that first the spiritual worship of God does not consist in external ceremonies, or any other kind of works whatsoever; and that no worship is legitimate unless it be so framed as to have for its only rule the will of him to whom it is performed. Men allow themselves to devise contrary to his command, he not only repudiates as void, but distinctly condemns" (*John Calvin, The Necessity of Reforming the Church*).

Notice Calvin says, "Worship is to be ordered according to rule of the one to whom it is performed."

A study of the full counsel of God is necessary to determine the outward expressions of worship. The debate is divided into two categories. The majority of Protestant churches assume the position that all expressions of worship are acceptable unless they are prohibited in Scripture. The minority report is that only the expressions commanded by God are acceptable. Although there are slight variations among the minority, they generally find prayer, offerings, singing Psalms and hymns, reading and preaching of the Word of God, the sacraments, and the benediction are necessary elements in public collective worship. Some churches are more specific. For instance, some churches believe the *Westminster Confession of Faith* outlines the biblical elements of worship. They are:

> Reading of the Scripture
> Sound preaching

Conscionable hearing of the Word
Obedience with understanding, faith, and reverence
Singing of psalms
Administration of sacraments
Religious oaths and vows
Solemn fastings
Thanksgivings upon special occasions
Prayer

Westminster applied the regulative principle to worship, which means that God has commanded in Scripture what He will accept in religious worship. There are specific qualifications for certain parts of Christian worship. Reading of Scriptures is not sufficient; rather they must be read with godly fear. Furthermore preaching is not enough. It must be sound preaching. That would disqualify much of what passes for preaching in churches in the present era. Apparently, *Westminster* does not believe that singing hymns is part of religious worship, because they only mention singing of Psalms. Even so, singing of Psalms is not enough. They must be sung with grace in the heart. Receiving the sacraments is not enough. It must be worthy receiving. Then there are special services for "special occasions, which are, in their several times and seasons, to be used in a holy and religious manner." If *Westminster* is wrong, then most of the evangelical church today is right. If *Westminster* is right, then most of the evangelical church today is wrong. The Bible is the final authority and Christians must be like the Bereans so that by searching the Scriptures the church will offer worship acceptable to the triune God, the object of Christian worship. I personally believe hymns may be part of Christian worship, if they are true to Holy Scripture. Unfortunately, many hymns are not true to Scripture and should not be used in worship. (*Doctrine of Sound Words*, by Martin Murphy, p. 130)

The only way to offer perfect worship is to offer worship to God through the perfect Mediator, the Lord Jesus Christ, by the power of the Holy Spirit.

36. I Apologize for My Apology

It has been said that the title of the book *My Christian Apology* is a play on words. The sub-title is *Apologetics Explained and Applied*. If it was a play on words then the author might lay claim to Jacques Derrida's postmodern deconstructionism. Since I am the author of *My Christian Apology* I apologize for my apology and denounce literary deconstructionism.

A few words about deconstructionism will suffice. The alleged father of literary deconstructionism, Jacques Derrida, explains (or does not explain) this concept. "The 'power' that language is capable of, the power that there is, as language or as writing, is that a singular mark should also be repeatable, iterable, as mark. It then begins to differ from itself sufficiently to become exemplary and thus involve a certain generality" (*Acts of Literature*). A very sophisticated suggestion from what appears to be the mind of a master sophist. The *Free Dictionary* turns the philosophical language into the vulgar language. "To a deconstructionist, meaning includes what is left out of the text or ignored or silenced by it. Because deconstruction is an attack on the very existence of theories and conceptual systems, its exposition by Derrida and others purposely resists logical definitions and explanations, opting instead for linear presentations based on extensive wordplay and puns." The result of this theory ends up in the literature class with a devastating effect. The subtle teaching is that the words of the speaker or writer have no absolute truth or meaning until it is deconstructed by the hearer or reader and reconstructed according to his or her world view.

When words were used to describe and define truth and reality, men and women expressed intelligent discourse. While many words are used on communication devices, there is little intelligent discourse. Postmodern theory illuminated "image is everything." Rational human discourse has been replaced with the postmodern ideas that absolute reality and truth does not exist.

> The postmodern culture is not a demon to be tamed, but a cultural milieu that must be replaced with a solid foundation that will grow a new culture. There must be an objective standard for the new culture, a standard that will survive cultural wars for the sake of its progeny. Today your most formidable enemy is not Washington D. C. as bad as they are. No, your most imposing enemy is the postmodern culture that feeds Washington D. C. If you don't remove the root that feeds the tree, you'll spend all your time pruning the tree. (*Constitutional Authority in a Postmodern Culture*, page 22)

"My Christian Apology" has no hidden meaning, doesn't need to be deconstructed, and it is certainly not necessary to reconstruct the meaning by discovering the meta-narratives that hide the intent of the author. The only word that would cause a Christian to flinch is "apology." The word apology comes from the Greek word transliterated *apologia*. The biblical meaning of *apologia* means to "give a defense." When Paul appeared before Felix in Acts 24 Paul said "I cheerfully make my defense." An apology has taken a new meaning. Webster says it may mean "a written or spoken expression of one's regret, remorse or sorrow." It has replaced the biblical way of reconciling relationships that is "forgive me."

Nominalism in medieval philosophy and postmodern deconstructionism in the 21st century simply disregards the notion that there is objective truth in the Christian world and life view. Reality is now considered a figment of the imagination. I write and I talk, but I find few readers and few listeners; However, I will continue to offer my Christian apology to defend my Christian world and life belief, D.V.

37. Church Growth

Why are some churches not growing and why are many other churches in decline? Is it the fault of the pastor(s)? Consider the life and ministry of a very influential preacher in North American history, Jonathan Edwards. He:

>1. Was a husband, father, and friend. "And no person of discernment could be conversant in the family, without observing, and admiring, the perfect harmony, and mutual love and esteem, that subsisted between them" (that is Mr. and Mrs. Edwards). His children treated him with respect and he was "fond. . .of welcoming the friend and stranger, and much as his house was a favorite place of resort. . .to ministers and others."

>2. Was an intellectual genius and of saintly character.

>3. Was a scholar with exceptional theological and philosophical acumen.

>4. Prepared each of his sermons with laborious care and each was a literary masterpiece.

>5. Participated in Great Awakening and spiritual revival in New England (1730-1740).

Even so, after ministering to the congregation at North Hampton for 23 years, Edwards was dismissed by the congregation.

Consider the life and ministry of Charles Spurgeon, one of the most famous preachers in England in the 19th century. What made Spurgeon so successful? If you could ask Spurgeon about his success, he would point to his people. There were two things his people did that brought success to Spurgeon's ministry. They introduced others to his ministry. They told others about this preacher. "You must come to hear him" they said, and so the crowds swelled and others told still others. (SPURGEON LIVED IN A TIME WHEN PEOPLE WERE HUNGRY FOR THE WORD OF GOD AND PREACHING WAS HELD IN HIGH REGARD.) They also prayed! A rather simple formula; a very biblical one, so I wonder why it's not widely practiced today?

Would a more distinguished theologian/preacher (Edwards or Spurgeon) cause the church to grow? I do not think so. The church will grow when God sends revival and reformation. Pray that God's professing people (the church) will seek to be reformed according to the Word of God, by the power of the Holy Spirit. Generally God uses people who are excited and zealous about the preaching of the Word of God. Church growth is not something Christians do, it is something Christians witness.

This article is not a visceral pleaser. In fact some people will conclude it is a useless harangue by an angry old man. Let me clarify a couple of my self-imposed assumptions. I'm not good at writing to touch the inner feelings of a therapeutically confused culture. My desire is to target the brain/mind. The brain is located in the upper portion of the human body and functions to process thought and memory by the use of neurons, synapses, and other electrical impulses. When the body dies, so does the brain. The mind, which is often used as a synonym for the brain, is metaphysical. It is a component of the soul. It will be around somewhere, forever. I'm writing this book to a truth seeking, intellectual, and rational brain/mind, but aware that all brain/minds are sinful. Therefore, some of them will understand what I write and others will resist it. As for "an angry old man" I am old and the Word of God instructs me to "Be angry and do not sin" (Ephesians 4:26). It does make me angry when I see the visible church falling into pieces, and professing Christians saying, "the church, the church, the church" (Jeremiah 7:3-4). Jeremiah's actual words were, "Thus says the Lord of hosts, the God of Israel: 'Amend your ways and your doings, and I will cause you to dwell in this place. Do not trust in these lying words, saying, 'The temple of the Lord, the temple of the Lord, the temple of the Lord are these."

The church growth movement, the mega-church concept, and various other exciting religious inventions charm professing

Christians with frills, thrills, and entertainment. These religious charms have captured the attention of churchmen around the world. "Marketing the church" has replaced the biblical concept of "making disciples." The Mega-church has replaced the biblical concept of a shepherd and the flock. It is important to realize that the church growth movement finds its most faithful followers referring to "contemporary worship" or talking about the "emerging church." These recent inventions spring forth from the church growth movement. This commentary is the result of my observation, research, and inquiry into the church growth movement. This is my critique of the movement and if correct, it is contrary to the doctrine and practice of the first thirty years of the church. My purpose in this chapter is to explain how modernity is inseparably related to the church growth movement.

The decline of the evangelical church may be attributed to any number of factors. However, two factors have significantly contributed to the decline. They are modernity and the church growth movement. The argument set forth is that although modernity has shaped the character of the evangelical church, the church growth movement is the driving force to implement the tools of modernity in the evangelical church.

38. Religious Activity is Killing the Professing Church

Religious activity in the United States has reached levels similar to the Roman Catholic Empire during the Dark Ages. History is replete with examples of nations touting their religious activity. One Bible verse keeps coming to mind; religious leaders are teaching people who are "always learning and never able to come to the knowledge of the truth" (2 Timothy 3:7). The latest fad in theology; the choicest religious seminar; the most popular celebrity are demonstrations of religious searching, but never able to come to the "knowledge of the truth." The Word, both living and written is the truth. Jesus said, "Everyone who is of the truth hears My voice" (John 18:37). Jesus also said, "And if I tell the truth, why do you not believe Me? He who is of God hears God's words; therefore you do not hear, because you are not of God" (John 8:46-47). Religion has replaced theology; popular false teachers have little or no interest in theology. They all claim Jesus, but which Jesus. The question is which Jesus is the real Jesus? Is it the Jesus, who is the human man with the divine idea? That is the teaching of Christian Science. Is it Jesus the first son that Jehovah God brought forth? That is the teaching of the Jehovah Witness organization. Is it the Jesus that was just like any other human except without original sin? That is the teaching of the Unification Church. They all give you Jesus, but they deny the deity of Jesus. Is it the Jesus that saves everyone? Is it the Jesus that wants to heal someone, if they will only believe? Which Jesus is the true Jesus? Do we need to start a new religious movement?

The church growth movement, the mega-church concept, and various other exciting religious inventions charm unbelievers and professing Christians with frills, thrills, and entertainment. These religious charms have captured the attention of churchmen around the world. "Marketing the church" has replaced the biblical concept of "making disciples." The Mega-church has replaced the biblical concept of a shepherd and the flock. It is important to realize that the church growth movement finds its most faithful followers referring to "contemporary worship" or talking about the "emerging church." These recent inventions spring forth from the church growth movement. Its follower's claim Jesus and they use numerous spoof texts to defend their religious activities.

The decline of the evangelical church may be attributed to any number of factors. However, three factors have significantly contributed to the decline. They are modernity, the church growth movement and postmodernity. The argument set forth is that although modernity has shaped the character of the evangelical church, the church growth movement is the driving force to implement the tools of modernity in the evangelical church. Postmodern concepts devised by the elite leaders in western civilization have now become part of western culture in such a way that denies absolute truth and reality. The evangelical church adopted modernity and married postmodernity. The result is astonishing: "Religious Activity is Killing the Professing Church." The only way to restore theology and sound biblical doctrine is to be reformed by the Word of God under the influence of the Holy Spirit.

39. Are You Being Reformed by the Word of God?

Revival is a work of God's Holy Spirit, but it shows itself through the vitality and renewal of what Jonathan Edwards calls "Religious Affections." He describes revival as a "renewed interest in the things of religion" [and a] vigorous upsurge of revivalism at the level of personal religion." Revival is not theoretical. It is an experience, not emotionalism, even though the emotions are affected, but more importantly the religious experience is visible and believable. The manifestation of these criteria seem to be absent among the majority of evangelicals at the beginning of this century. Why is there no revival in the evangelical church?

Reformation (the recovery of biblical truth) will always precede revival. First, one must acknowledge the authority of Scripture. The central teaching of Scripture states that a right standing with God comes by faith alone and that faith itself is a gift of God, as salvation itself is a gift from God. What are the primary means for announcing this gift from God? The primary means are preaching the Word of God and teaching; preaching is the instrument of reformation and revival.

Richard Hofstadter in his Pulitzer Prize winning book, *Anti-Intellectualism in American Life,* points out that "sermons are not producing any noticeable change in the lives of Christians in North America." In comparing sermons today with the sermons preached 200 years ago in this country Hofstadter said, "Puritan sermons combined philosophy, piety, and scholarship. . . The clergy assumed responsibility for a literate culture. Such an assumption shows the gulf between the profound substance of Puritan sermons and some of the modern inspirational pep talks which pass for sermons."

Preaching has moved from substantial reflections on the character and nature of God to a forum on "How to...do things, have things, and be successful." The "How to Gospel" has bankrupted the evangelical church. The biblical gospel is almost extinct and is certainly offensive to the ears of most evangelicals.

"We are accused of rash and impious innovation, for having ventured to propose any change at all on the former state of the Church" (*The Necessity of Reforming the Church*, by John Calvin, Works, vol. 1, p.125). Calvin used two interesting words that aptly describe reformation. The word "innovation" from the Latin word *innovare*, which means "to renew," was needed in the day of Calvin and it is needed today. The church does not need a new gospel or a new way to worship, but it does need to restore the gospel and the orthodox way to worship which has been trampled upon over the past couple of centuries. Innovation describes the work of reformation and change describes the result of reformation.

Michael Horton argues that "theology, not morality, is the first business on the church's agenda of reform, and the church, not society, is the first target of divine criticism" (*Beyond Culture Wars*, by Michael Horton). Innovation begins with theology and ends with theology. Paul the apostle said "I press on to take hold of that for which Christ Jesus took hold of me." Paul strived for an understanding of righteousness, peace and the knowledge of Jesus Christ, which is essentially and practically theological. Paul's innovation rested squarely on a theological framework. A reformer is innovative only when he or she has a passion for believing and living according to God's standard as he or she is enabled to believe and live by the power of the Holy Spirit.

The meaning of reformation and thus what it means to be a reforming Christian, has been forgotten, because the evangelical church, the carrier of the Reformation, has turned her back on the foundational doctrines of the Christian faith. True reformation is the church being reformed by the Word of God. The evangelical church has replaced the law and the gospel with human-centered structures that meet "felt needs," those that are "user-friendly", and are "seeker sensitive."

At the beginning of the Reformation Martin of Basle came to the knowledge of the truth of the gospel, but he was afraid to make a public confession. He wrote these words on a leaf of parchment: "O most merciful Christ, I know that I can be saved only by the merit of thy blood. Holy Jesus, I acknowledge thy sufferings for me. I love thee! I love thee!" He removed a stone from the wall of his chamber and hid it. It was not discovered until a hundred years later.

About the same time Martin Luther discovered the truth and he openly confessed: "My Lord has confessed me before men; I will not shrink from confessing Him before kings." The Reformation continued and we remember Martin Luther for his devotion to innovation and change, but what about Martin of Basle? Who was the reformer?

Innovation is that aspect of reformation that seeks to recover the integrity and dignity of the Christian religion. Our forefathers suffered and died for the integrity of the gospel and with dignity they have passed on to us the torch of reformation. John Calvin left us with these words and I leave them with you: "But be the issue what it may, we will never repent of having begun and of having proceeded thus far. We will die, but in death even be conquerors...because we know that our blood will be as seed to propagate the Divine truth which men now despise" (*The Necessity of Reforming the Church*, by John Calvin, Vol. 1, p. 234.).

40. Biblical Reformation Is Not Neutral

Although I've lectured and written on the doctrine of reformation, I don't think I've explained the principle of reformation using the life of Josiah the King of Judah. The word reformation denotes a change from one way of thinking or acting to another way of thinking or acting. Reformers are agents for change in a specific discipline of a culture. For instance, there are political reformers who work toward reforming the governance of a culture. There are social reformers, moral reformers, cultural reformers, religious reformers and others who engage in the process of reformation. Unfortunately, the reformers mentioned in the previous sentence do not have an ultimate authority.

Biblical reformation is more specific and has an ultimate authority. Biblical reformation refers to the church of every generation being reformed by the Word of God; It is the ultimate authority for reformation in the church. Biblical reformation is not a *kairotic* event. A *kairotic* event refers to a specific event in time or a particular point in time that has great significance for the rest of time. (The birth of Jesus Christ was a *kairotic* event.) Biblical reformation is a chronological engagement. Biblical reformation is not just about changes. Biblical reformation is a process that leads Christians to understand the nature and character of God in contrast to sinful man. It is a process that directs Christians to love the nature and character of God, so that their passion is to worship Him. For clarification, the term "biblical reformation" does not refer to any aspect of the order of salvation. Christians may be reformed by the Word of God. Unbelievers cannot be reformed by the Word of God until God calls them and gives them new life in Jesus Christ.

Reformation is not the same as revival. Reformation for Christians is simply the process of rediscovering or even discovering biblical truth. Revival is the expression and practice of being reformed by the Word of God and empowered by the Holy Spirit.

Two essential and fundamental concepts were evident during the 16th century Protestant Reformation. First the church was being reformed by the Word of God. The church was passive since it was being reformed, but it was active by always reforming. Each generation of the church must be reformed by the Word of God. It is the process of recovering the correct view and understanding the full counsel of God, especially the doctrines of sin, salvation, and worship.

Jonathan Edwards made the following comment during the reformation at the Northampton congregation. "At a time when God manifests himself in such a great work for his church, there is no such thing as being neuter." Edwards is right. Professing Christians cannot be neutral, but there are obvious reasons for no reformation in church:

> 1. Natural man cannot be reformed; natural man does not receive the things of the Spirit of God, for they are foolishness to him; nor can he know them, because they are spiritually discerned" (1 Corinthians 2:14).
>
> 2. Wicked men will not seek reformation (Genesis 19:12-29).
>
> 3. Ignorance often prevents reformation; This is illustrated by the disciples on the road to Emmaus and their ignorance of the Scriptures (Luke 24:13-35). "Did not our heart burn within us while He talked with us on the road, and while He opened the Scriptures to us" (Luke 24:32).
>
> 4. Professing Christians who have no interest in truth have no interest in reformation. "Run to and fro through the streets of Jerusalem; See now and know; and seek in her open places if you can find a man, If there is anyone who executes judgment who seeks the truth and I will pardon her" (Jeremiah 5:1).

The church always needs to be reforming because Satan and his entourage of followers try to deceive the followers of Christ that they do not need reformation (Matthew 4:1-4). The church always needs reforming because sinful hearts and hands are inclined to abuse true worship and allow false worship to enter into the church. Tradition often becomes an object of worship, thus the need to be reformed by the Word of God.

The words reform and reformation remind people of changes. Some people don't like changes. Some people like to change everything. Biblical reformation is not merely about changes. Biblical reformation is a process that leads professing Christians to understand the nature and character of God, a process that leads them to love the nature and character of God, so their passion is to worship Him. Reforming worship means rediscovering the centrality of Jesus Christ as the object of worship by the church.

The church that is not reforming will devolve its corruption to the next generation. The 17th century Puritan scholar, Francis Turretin, said the call to reformation is such that "a man is bound to purge his faith and worship of all the errors and superstitions by which it could be corrupted so that he may retain religion pure from every stain" (*Institutes of Elenctic Theology*, Vol. 3, p. 217).

How is it possible for a man to purge his faith and worship of all errors and superstitions? Is it possible to remove all the corruption that comes with the sinful heart? Can our religion be pure from every stain? For certain we dismiss the idea of perfection in faith, practice and worship. What Turretin has in mind is the standard to which we judge all of life including faith and worship. That standard is the Word of God. Our religion will never be completely pure from every stain, but if there is any purity at all, it will be the result of our understanding the Word of God.

One of the best accounts of biblical reformation may be found in 2 Chronicles chapters 34 and 35. During the reign of Manesseh and his son, Amon, there were all sorts of false worship, and impure religion. The enthronement of Josiah as king of Judah brought a sudden and dramatic change to the church of his day. Josiah started seeking God, which is the first step to reformation. It worked for Josiah and it'll work for you. Josiah started to seek the Lord in the 8th year of his reign and within 10 years his own personal reformation began to have a public influence.

In the 18th year of Josiah's reign he ordered Shaphan the scribe, Maaseiah the governor, and Joah the recorder to repair the house of the Lord. When these men consulted Hilkiah the high priest, he reported that he had found the Book of the Law of the Lord given by

Moses. Today we call it the Bible. If Hilkiah, the high priest, had not been busy working for reformation, he would not have found the Bible.

Now someone may think that this portion of God's Word is irrelevant. Someone may think we have Bibles everywhere. We haven't lost our Bibles. Oh yes, we are in danger of losing the Bible, but not as a volume of literature. Let me put it another way: We are in danger of losing the Word of God. I'll mention some of the dangers.

1. It is possible to lose the Word of God because of indifference.

2. It is possible to lose the Word of God because the Scriptures are not studied. (I didn't say read, I said studied.)

3. If professing Christians despise the preaching of the Word of God, the Word of God may be lost.

4. It is possible to lose the Word of God because it is considered irrelevant.

Whether we lose the Word of God through neglect, disbelief, or disobedience, we are brought to the same end. Sin, vice, and misery are the natural results of losing the Word of God. Without the Word of God men will hate true worship. Without the Word of God false worship will replace true worship. Without the Word of God the church has no purpose or understanding of true worship.

The rediscovery of the Book of the Law (The Word of God) found in 2 Chronicles 34:14-22 is a bit curious. Hilkiah found the Word of God and gave it to Shaphan. Shaphan was a scribe. The duty of the scribe was to write legal documents for the king or any other work that required writing skills. Hilkiah was a priest. The priest, according to the Word of God in Deuteronomy 33:10, was to teach Israel the law of God and lead the people in temple worship.

Who should have read the book of the law when it was discovered? Hilkiah the priest, but he didn't. Why? He had the Word of God, but was not being reformed by the Word of God. The king instructed 5 men (men mind you) to get a word from the Lord, but where did those men go? They went to a prophetess, rather than following the directions for discovering God's will prescribed in the Word of God.

The Urim and Thummim were to be used for discovering God's will. The Word of God explains: "And you shall put in the breastplate of judgment the Urim and the Thummim, and they shall be over Aaron's heart when he goes in before the Lord. So Aaron shall bear the judgment of the children of Israel over his heart before the Lord continually" (Exodus 28:30; Ezra 2:63; Numbers 27:21).

The nature of the objects are uncertain, but one thing is for certain, they were to be worn by the priests, who were men. Urim and Thummim were to be used to obtain God's judgment on a matter.

Acting contrary to the Word of God, what did Shaphan and Hilkiah do? Rather than being reformed by the Word of God these men did what they had been doing their entire lifetime; they leaned on their own understanding instead of obeying Scripture. Even King Josiah understood that the wrath of the Lord was poured out because their fathers had not kept the Word of the Lord. The church ought to take heed to the example of King Josiah and seek to be reformed by the Word of God. Don't let tradition dictate the doctrine of Scripture. Don't let the culture you live in be your standard for faith, life, and worship.

The result of reformation will have two significant results. First, being reformed by the Word of God has a universal dimension. King Josiah gathered all the elders of Judah and Jerusalem, with all the people of Judah and Jerusalem, both great and small. Secondly, being reformed by the Word of God is a very serious matter. The king and all the people made a vow.

Then the king stood in his place and made a covenant before the LORD, to follow the LORD, and to keep His commandments and His testimonies and His statutes with all his heart and all his soul, to perform the words of the covenant that were written in this book. And he made all who were present in Jerusalem and Benjamin take a stand. So the inhabitants of Jerusalem did according to the covenant of God, the God of their fathers (2 Chronicles 34:31-32).

Being reformed by the Word of God will touch every part of the soul - the mind, emotions, and will. Once a child of God discovers the truth of the full counsel of God intellectually, it will have an effect on his or her decisions and there will be an outward manifestation of his or her love for truth.

Finally, when God's people have been reformed by the Word of God, they will stick close to His Word throughout their lives. When the Holy Spirit has done His work and changes the hearts of His people, then being reformed by the Word of God will continue throughout their lives. Personal reformation that extends to the church collectively will purge our faith and worship of error and corruption.

If Christians are not being reformed by the Word of God, they will find themselves corrupted by the ways of the culture around them. The corruption will find its place in worship. In due time corrupt worship will send the church to Babylon. If you are being reformed by the Word of God, you will rediscover again and again the object of your salvation and the centrality of worship.

41. Clarion Call to the Church

The Fall of the year is when Protestant Christians should be reminded of their Reformation heritage and a few actually begin to search for a new Reformation. Unfortunately the Christmas holiday consumes their attention, so religious reformation is soon forgotten. Other Christians are content to search for spooks, witches, devils, and demons that hide behind the corner ready to frighten you. Actually they are waiting in the department stores for you to buy them, so you will have a costume for Halloween. It is with great delight that I remind Christians the significance of October 31st is not found in the holiday we call Halloween.

On the eve of All Saints Day, October 31, 1517, at twelve o'clock, Dr. Martin Luther went to the door of the castle church and posted ninety five theses on the church door. This was the normal process used to ask for an academic disputation (a debate) on a particular theological question. Luther had an irresistible compulsion to resolve the question of indulgences. The manner he chose was widely practiced and a regular feature of university life at that time.

The title of the theses was a *Disputation to Explain the Virtue of Indulgences* (Commonly referred to as the 95 Theses). Luther was careful to explain that "They are no protest against the Pope and the Roman Church, or any of her doctrine, not even against indulgences, but only against their abuses."

No one responded to the challenge for debate, but God heard the cries of Martin Luther along with other professors and students at Whittenberg. Rather than debating the issues, the Pope took offense to Luther and set out to destroy Martin Luther. It was time for reformation (recovery of biblical truth) and God brought it about by using the least likely man, Dr. Martin Luther, and the least likely doctrine, indulgences.

The church has celebrated the Reformation on October 31st for the past 500 years. It is the birthday of the Protestant Church. It is the Protestant Church, because a "protest" was made against false teaching. The Protestant Church is now lost in the maze of denominations and false teaching that has accumulated for over 500 years.

It is time for Christians to recover or discover the meaning of reformation. The definition is simple, but engaging in reformation takes a resolute mind. Reformation is the recovery or discovery of biblical truth based on the full counsel of God! If God grants reformation, courageous, intelligent, and devoted Christians will be His instruments. Christians must be willing to protest against the abuses and false teaching in the church. Not many, if any, are willing to take the financial loss to protest. Instead they schedule a seminar, get a few celebrity speakers to explain reformation, and charge the participants $119.00 for attending the seminar.

Luther's protest began by saying: "In the desire and with the purpose of elucidating the truth, a disputation will be held on the underwritten propositions at Wittenberg, under the presidency of the Reverend Father Martin Luther, Monk of the Order of St. Augustine, Master of Arts and of Sacred Theology, and ordinary Reader of the same at that place. He therefore asks those who cannot be present, and discuss the subject with us orally, to do so by letter in their absence." Now, as in the day of Luther, discussing and debating the doctrinal and theological issues and submitting to the authority of Scripture are the means we should use in our search for reformation.

Some of the greatest enemies of the church are those para-church organizations who use the church like a leech feeding on its prey. However, not all para-church ministries pull the church down. Some devote themselves to the work of preserving the orthodoxy of the Christian religion. Reformation is a joint venture and not an individual agenda.

The struggle for identity has driven many ministers and laymen away from working for Reformation in the church. They have retreated into the chaotic worlds of pragmatism, consumerism and relativism. Many ungodly worldviews have them trapped in a postmodern agenda. I challenge you as the Word of God does, "not to be conformed to this world, but be transformed by the renewing of your mind" (Romans 12:2).

I pray God will motivate and inspire a new Martin Luther or John Calvin, or John Knox to stress the importance of reformation, for without it the evangelical church will continue to slide into the abyss. I haven't completely given up, but I don't see any widespread effort for reformation in my life time. But, then perhaps the Holy Spirit of God will marvelously bring about a new Reformation that I may witness it before I die.

42. Is Your Conscience Held Captive to the Word of God?

The autumn days remind me of change and anticipation of the long winter ahead. Most people think of hunting season, football, or a visit to the mountains to see the beauty of the changing seasons. This change of seasons reminds me of a most significant day to celebrate. The special day is October 31st. It was on this day 501 years ago that Martin Luther challenged the church with his 95 theses.

Luther never intended to start a new church or to divide the Roman Catholic Church. Luther simply wanted to see reform within the church. He saw the condition of the church and wanted to debate some theological issues that seemed un-orthodox for Christianity. Although others paved the way before him, most historians credit October 31, 1517 as the beginning of the Protestant Reformation. The Protestant Church was a product of the 16th century Reformation in Europe.

By the end of the 20th century, the Protestant Church had lost its meaning and purpose. The word protestant is derived from the Latin word *protestari* which, has the root meaning "to protest." James Davidson Hunter, Professor of Sociology and Religious Studies at the University of Virginia, correctly assessed the historical perspective. He said that "the Protestant Reformation in the 16th century created one of the most fundamental cultural divisions in the history of Western Civilization." He goes on to say, "the practical efforts of the Reformation have, at least in the U.S. context, become both politically and culturally defunct." The Protestant Church is no longer protesting against the world and life views that prevail within the halls of evangelicalism.

Martin Luther protested against the deviation from the fundamental teachings of Christianity. He argued that the church must return to the doctrine of *sola fide* (faith alone). *Sola fide* teaches that man is declared righteous in the sight of God by an act of God. The contrary heresy was that man was made righteous, a prevailing doctrine in the modern evangelical church. The authority by which

Luther would argue for the doctrine of "justification by faith alone" was *sola scriptura* (by Scripture alone). Luther realized that Holy Scripture is the ultimate authority for the church. From these "protests" (by faith alone, by Scripture alone, and others) the Protestant Church was born.

Reformation, in biblical categories, refers to a recovery of biblical truth. Reformation as a principle has occurred many times in the Old Testament and in the history of the New Testament church. Reformation is occasional, in an iterative sense, and has no geographical bounds. For example, there was reformation during the reign of King Josiah of Judah, during the return of the Jews from the Babylonian exile and during the life and ministry of Jesus, who was the most significant reformer of all times.

There is a difference between reformation and revival. While reformation is the recovery (or in some cases the discovery) of biblical truth, revival is the process of bringing biblical reformation into human experience. Hosea's famous charge was, "return to the Lord" thus it was reformation and revival simultaneously.

The Latin phrase used to describe true reformation is *ecclesia reformata semper est reformanda*. "The church being reformed is always reforming" is more than a motto for the church. It ought to be the world and life view of the church. Every generation must recover the truth or discover the truth in order to be reformed by the Word of God. However, something has been amiss for several generations.

Why did God use Martin Luther to introduce the 16th Century Reformation? It was not because Luther had more theological acumen or more charisma than others in the church. Luther was convicted by the Holy Spirit and unafraid of any man. Luther was not worried about his support being cut off by the church. He was not afraid of members leaving the church. He didn't cherish his denomination or love his tradition. He was ready to be God's man at any cost, even his life.

While Luther was on trial he was asked to deny his teachings and books. His reply was (in part): "Unless I am convinced by the testimony of the Scriptures or by clear reason, I am bound by the Scriptures I have quoted, and my conscience is captive to the Word of God."

When your conscience is held captive to the Word of God, reformation is inevitable! Revival will naturally follow. Please help us find a Martin Luther at the beginning of the 21st century.

43. Hope and Vision for Reformation

Thomas Edison said, "restlessness and discontent are the first necessities of progress." I find myself restless and discontent with the obvious decline of the true Christian religion as it is defined by the Word of God. My restless and discontent soul drives me to ask myself the question: Martin, do you have a vision and hope for reformation in the church?

If you think I have a passion for reformation, then I'm guilty. My passion is not for the return of the 16th century Reformation or the return of the "good ole days" (which were not good at all). My passion is for reformation with a little "r." Our 16th century Reformation forefathers were not satisfied with the Reformation, they wanted reformation. They understood the biblical concept of reformation, which demands the recovery or discovery of biblical truth. The recovery of the law and gospel is the foundation for reformation in the church. The Reformation fathers were God's instruments to recover the truth in the whole counsel of God. They saw reformation as an indicative in the present tense and in the passive voice. It was a matter of fact they were being reformed by the Word of God under the power of the Holy Spirit. They were active participants, but they were being acted upon by the Holy Spirit and the Word of God.

This brings us to a point of self-examination. Are we being reformed by the Word of God through the illuminating power of the Holy Spirit or do we try to reform the Word of God according the power of darkness? The evidence indicates a strong move among reformed and evangelical churches toward reforming the Word of God rather than being reformed by it.

The cause of the epidemic abuse cannot be easily traced to any particular discipline or lack thereof. However, there are several foundational philosophical dynamics at work. When the 16th century Reformation began, the parochialism of Rome was replaced by evangelicalism, which is truly universal. While the church was liberated from parochialism, there was the sacrifice of unity for

Musing Christian Principles

diversity. Although diversity is not sinful in essence, it affords the opportunity for the birth and nurture for private agendas and ultimately individualism.

The cultural milieu has been and still is in the process of change. The light of modernity begins to fade as postmodern thinkers begin to emerge. Orthodox belief systems are being challenged. Historical revisionism and deconstructionism have trickled down from the intellectual elites to the rest of us. Theology has been replaced with religion. Intellectual pursuit has been replaced with the "dumbing down of Christians." Sacrifice has been replaced by prosperity seekers. Tradition has been replaced by the contemporary. Tradition may become sin, but it is not essentially and necessarily sinful. Tradition is important to provide stability to an orthodox belief system.

Christians rightly ask, "What's the solution?" The solution is a process called reformation. The Word of God rather than our preferences must be the basis of our belief system. Confessional standards must be maintained with integrity and dignity. A passion for truth must find a place of honor at the debate table. The aggregate of these principles equals reformation in the church.

What we believe, what we know, and what we practice will set the agenda for reformation in the church. On the other hand corruption and a continuing descent away from biblical truth will steal away the hope and vision for reformation. It is my hope and vision that pastors, theologians, and laymen will find a passion for reformation in their individual soul. The expression of that passion will be the seed for revival in the church.

The mandate to carry the gospel to the ends of the earth is abundantly clear in Scripture. However, in recent church history men have devised many pragmatic schemes to "win the lost." The side show mentality has found its way into the church with astounding success and with it a plan for people to make a decision for Christ. Now I ask you, with all the evangelistic success over the past 100 years, why is the church so sick? The answer is simple. The powers to be in the church failed to teach reformation principles, thus they forgot to recover the truth of the law and gospel. The gospel went forth without the law. A sinner cannot believe and receive the gospel without the law preceding the gospel. An appreciation of God's grace can be seen only in the light of God's wrath. Remove God's wrath and the gospel is worthless. The hope and vision for reformation will give the church hope and vision for making disciples and a new order for personal Christian growth.

It is time for reforming reformers to step forward and tell the local church that the church must be reformed by the Word of God. You may be the one person who will inspire the congregation with the spirit of reformation. It is my prayer that your hope and vision for the church is reformation. I still have hope and vision for the church being reformed according to the Word of God, by the power of the Holy Spirit.

44. Judgment For the Unreformed Church

The word reform denotes a change from one way of life to another way of life. The book of Jonah depicts the true nature of reformation in the most universal sense. There may be a few preachers who talk about reformation, but they do not appear to take reformation very serious. When they do talk about reformation they are often concerned with constraint and circumscriptions that limit reformation. Let me make it clear that when I use the word reformation, I have biblical reformation in mind. Biblical reformation is the discovery or either the recovery of biblical truth. Since reformation is the recovery of biblical truth, we should hasten to bring it about. Recovering the truth of the law and gospel is ultimately important for the survival of the church, because such recovery integrates dignity and moral standards.

Look at the little ones among us. While some of us are getting ready to die, they're getting ready to live. What will we devolve on the shoulders of our children and grandchildren if we do not seriously and sincerely seek reformation in the church, thus affecting every area of life including our religious, familial, social, economic, and political lives? An insincere reformation is no reformation at all.

The book and life of Jonah reflect the principles necessary for reformation in the church that will lead to reformation in the culture. Being reformed by the Word of God is necessary to grasp the substance of life and eternity. To ignore reformation is dangerous indeed, because without reformation God's wrath will be provoked.

> When you begat children and grandchildren and have grown old in the land, and act corruptly and make a carved image in the form of anything, and do evil in the sight of the Lord your God to provoke Him to anger, I call heaven and earth to witness against you this day.... (Deuteronomy 4:25)

Doing evil provokes God to anger. From 1450 B.C. to 600 B.C. the people of God provoked God to the point that His glory departed from the temple in Jerusalem. It was symbolic of God's favorable presence leaving the people that professed to believe Him.

The people in Sodom tried neutrality. It didn't work. When the wicked men of Sodom were told of the eminent destruction they just couldn't believe it was true. The nearness, the uncertainty, greatness and eternity of God's punishment and wrath doesn't seem dreadful or miserable for the unreformed man. Natural man cannot be reformed and wicked men will not be reformed, but those whom God has called to Himself can and must seek reformation. The choice is simple: reformation or judgment.

The reformation in Ninevah was not permanent. Every generation must seek reformation according to the Word of God. Every Christian and every generation must rediscovery the truth of the Word of God, so the beauty, majesty, and dignity of God will be evident in the church.

After Jonah's personal reformation he went to preach reformation to the whole city of Nineveh or to put it in other terms Jonah preached to a culture unfamiliar with the true and living God. Jonah went through the streets of Nineveh preaching a very simple, but very persuasive sermon: "Yet forty days, and Nineveh shall be overthrown." Apparently Jonah's preaching was very powerful and very convincing, because the whole city repented in sackcloth and ashes.

The repentance at Nineveh was universal and was occasioned by their faith in God. The unexpected, but sudden reformation at Nineveh began with the people and very quickly reached the heads of state. The undeniable truth from the book of Jonah is that the reformation at Nineveh saved that city from God's impending judgment. "Then God saw their works, that they turned from their evil way; and God relented from the disaster that He had said He would bring upon them and He did not do it (Jonah 3:10)." The sinful people at Nineveh were about to have the wrath of God poured out upon them. But God showed mercy after the people of Nineveh were reformed.

What we learn from Jonah and Nineveh is that reformation and the people turning from their evil ways averts God's threatened judgment. Not only from Jonah, God spoke through the prophet Jeremiah and said, "The instant I speak concerning a nation and concerning a kingdom, to pluck up, to pull down, and to destroy it, if that nation against whom I have spoken turns from its evil, I will relent of the disaster that I thought to bring upon it (Jeremiah 18:7)."

God not only calls the church to reformation, but God calls nations to reform. The church should be the light on the hill. Once the church has recovered the truth of God's grace, the church must then take that truth to the culture. Our present national sins should be of great concern to the church. Today God's people feel the threats of every international, national, and local crisis that erupts. We sense the coming economic calamity. We see the moral catastrophe that accompanies a form of godliness among so many professing Christians.

The people of Nineveh believed the Word of God. This is the central principle of reformation "they believed the Word of God." Then they fasted. Like Jonah, you'll have to experience personal reformation first. Rediscover God's truth. The light of God's truth will light up a passion for reformation that will work itself out as a revival.

The well intentioned Christian may say: "We know of God's impending judgment, but preaching God's judgment will chase people away and we'll never get to save them." It is correct that the church cannot save anyone. God saves and He uses His word to convict sinners of their sins. When the "Lord opened her (Lydia's) heart to heed the things spoken" she was able to believe and seek reformation from the written Word by the inward work of the Holy Spirit (Acts 16:14).

The majority of the church and most of our nation has not given attention to the terrible threats of God. A few sermons have been preached about reformation and the imminent dangers if the church continues unreformed. Those sermons have largely been ignored. God is angry with the gross hypocrisy and the great heresies that plague the professing church. The church will do well to listen to God's threat of judgment. The church will do well to cut out all the talk about reformation, and stop amusing themselves with egocentric worship. Useless talk and self-worship will find its end in God's judgment. The present unreformed church simply refuses to preach the simplicity of God's grace, man's sinful condition and in particular the doctrine of God's salvation.

The church must recover the full counsel of God for reformation in the church extending to the culture. Judgment of the unreformed church may be prevented, if the church will:

1. Seek God's counsel from His Word
2. Hide God's Word in the heart's mind
3. Declare God's Word without shame
4. Delight in the Word of God and never forget it

Reformation is the recovery of biblical truth.

Natural man cannot recover biblical truth.

Wicked men will not recover biblical truth.

God's covenant people are the only instruments of reformation.

Will we do any less than the Ninevites?

Will we believe?

Will we repent?

If so, God may relent from the disaster that is coming upon us!

45. Cultural Dilemma

The identity of a cultural dilemma is the necessary diagnosis for cultural recovery. The prognosis requires the imperative. The introduction of postmodernity to the American culture paved the way to this neo-dark age. The sophists work covertly, but deliberately building worldviews contrary to rational thought. The sophisticated postmodern deconstructionist scrupulously avoids the rules for intelligent human discourse. They have decimated the Christian world view with the slight of tongue and literary sophistication.

Although I do not agree wholeheartedly with Alasydair MacIntyre's views in his book *After Virtue* he did awaken me to the dominant forces influencing the 20th century world views in the United States. The dominant forces are the manager, the therapist, and the aesthete. They are the top shelf of the socio-economic strata in this country. MacIntyre alleges that "truth has been displaced as a value and replaced by psychological effectiveness" (*After Virtue*, p. 31).

The imperative necessary to recover a biblical world and life view will require spokesmen who believe in the basic rules of intelligent human discourse. For over a century the evangelical church cheerfully gave up the use of rational inquiry in the discipline of apologetics. Even more serious was the abandonment of natural law. Reasonable recovery along with a new standard in scholarly inquiry is necessary for the survival of a rational culture.

I believe most of the western world is in transit between any number of major philosophical influences. I wrote a paper over ten years ago arguing that metaphysical inquiry had been neutralized by postmodern thought. Evidence favors my theory at the beginning of the 21st century that metaphysical inquiry is nearly dead.

Cultural recovery means a recovery of truth. When I use the word truth, I have in mind a conceptual idea that truth is reality and that truth affirms itself aesthetically, reasonably, and sensibly. Truth reveals itself in beauty, wisdom, rationality, and in the world of sense experience. Does that mean that ethics and morals are exempt from the meaning established for truth? Absolutely not and in fact an ethical system and the functions of morality are manifested (not established) in a reasonable world with aesthetically and sensibly derived propositions.

Cultural recovery will require a passion for truth. We have to remember how far we've fallen into the arms of modernity and postmodern theory. We have to remember that our children, with rare exceptions, have not understood or even studied rules of logic. We have to remember that our children have been taught that truth is relative. We have to remember that our children have learned to make decisions based on emotional subjectivism, rather than rational objectivism. Professor David Wells said "it is not theology alone in which I am interested but theology that is driven by a passion for truth." By analogy, I can say the same about culture, politics, or economics. We must have a passion for truth.

Cultural recovery will require a passion for absolute truth. The neo-dark age before us is prefaced with the postmodern interpretation theory called deconstructionism. It is nothing more than an interpretative device that allows one to deconstruct written literary forms and reconstruct them so that they become meaningful to the interpreter. This is not the same as relativism, because the meaning is absolute for the interpreter, but it certainly seems kin to relativism to me. How many times have I heard someone say that "truth is relative." Truth cannot be relative. Truth is absolute. Truth is absolutely absolute.

We must understand and teach our children the difference between truth and error, so they may understand the difference between freedom and tyranny. Even the social compact theorist, John, Locke, said "Tyranny is the exercise of power beyond right." If we do not understand what is "right" we will ultimately be the subjects of tyranny. I cannot say often enough that our Christian forefathers were men of truth. They realized that truth was an attribute of God and a gift to the human race. May we all look to the Lord for His divine decree, as we work toward cultural recovery?

46. Egalitarianism and Racial Ignorance

This morning a young black female made this statement on a nationally televised news program: "You have to legislate equality in this country." If this type of ignorant gibberish gains popularity the appearance of atheism will prevail. It is already prominent. Those who suppress the truth have a worthless mind (Romans 1:18-32). Liberation theology has served as a conduit to popularize "equality." Traditional intellectual philosophy has been replaced by social postmodern theory. The only hope for the next generation is "Hold fast the pattern of sound words which you have heard from me [the Apostle Paul], in faith and love which are in Christ Jesus" (2 Timothy 1:13). I have these words for anyone with a reasonable mind: God did not ordain equality and strife, God ordained order and harmony. I wish everyone in this country, especially Christians, had the opportunity to read my comments on egalitarianism and racial ignorance.

The classical meaning of race and racism has been practically effaced by the literary jargon of the 19th and 20th century. The common use of the word race allegedly refers to a class of people related by blood, ethnic similarities, traditions, et al. It has become a common practice to add the English suffix "ism" to caricature a word to the degree of a world and life view. Then racism becomes a term meaning the supreme exaltation of a race of people. The consequence would be the hatred for a different ethnic group. The *imago Dei* (the image of God) is a natural resident for all human beings according to Christian theology. R. L. Dabney's Systematic Theology posits, "we learn that man, unlike all lower creatures, was formed in the 'image of God – after His likeness.' The general idea here is obviously, that there is a resemblance of man to God."

There is a certain ubiquity associated with the term racism. To show the shallow rational and mental effort put into defining words we only have to turn to *Webster's Dictionary*. It describes racism as "a belief that human races have distinctive characteristics that determine their respective cultures usually involving the idea that one's own race is superior and has the right to rule others." Then Webster defines race as "a group of persons related by common descent, blood, or heredity." According to Webster there is a difference in races when using the term "race" but when using "racism" the subjectivity shifts only to "a belief" that there are differences in races. God created one race, the human race, but because of sin they are divided into various ethnic groups. The mass media, powerful politicians, and elusive educators have successfully duped Americans into believing that definitions to words are unnecessary. We live at a time when ignorance hides under the charm of scholarship and true education is condemned by uneducated scholars. Anti-intellectualism has been crowned queen of the public square.

The greatest gift God gave the human race was a rational mind. (Please note: The greatest gift God gave the children of God is the grace of salvation through the Lord Jesus Christ.) An uneducated man may use his rational faculties. However, an educated man may suppress his rational faculties. An uneducated man may employ principles of logic while the educated man may employ the principles of confusion. We have cultural elites treating words with contempt and stirring up confusion. The sad effect will eventually show its face. One day people will learn, maybe too late, that words are meaningful. Then many will look back and realize theological and philosophical principles relating to life and culture should not have been ignored.

The contemporary church has adopted the imaginary assumption that God ordained an egalitarian undefined people called human beings. In so doing the church ignores the basic principle of taxonomy found in Genesis chapter one. God not only classified His creation, He ordered the division of nations, boundaries, and an inheritance by separating them into their various lands (Genesis 10). They were nations with various ethnic and cultural distinctions. When we avoid the distinction of nations, ethnic groups, and cultural milieus (popularly misinterpreted as racism) we promote the sin of egalitarianism. I need only to remind you that the amalgamation of the races was a sin against God (Genesis 11). The Bible teaches that it is a sin to despise or hate another person for any reason, especially because of their natural birth. The sin is not "racism" but that of pride, envy, and murder. It is humanism that has reversed God's plan. It is humanism with its beloved children (multi-culturalism, despotism, and the one world order) that say "let us build ourselves a city and a tower reaching to the heavens; let us make a name for ourselves."

The passion of every human being is the desire to be equal to God. It began with the first two people representing the human race. They were charmed with the idea they could "be like God" (Genesis 3:5). Natural man says, "I am and there is no one else besides me" (Isaiah 47:10). Egalitarianism is a world view popularized by the war cry of the French Revolution, " Liberty, Equality, and Fraternity." Egalitarianism or the rarely used term, ultimate equalism, is wicked to the core. The human race is only equal in terms of, "all are sinners." R. L. Dabney rightly declared,

> The extreme claim of equality is false and iniquitous. For out of the wide natural diversities of sex and of character must arise a wide difference of natural relations between individuals and the State. To attempt to bestow identical franchises upon all thus appears to be unjust, and, indeed, impossible.

There are universal natural distinctions found in human beings. However, he also believed,

> There is a natural moral equality between all men, in that all are generically men. All [people] have a rational, responsible and immortal destiny, and are inalienably entitled to pursue it; all [people] are morally related alike to God, the common Father; and all have equitable title to the protection of the laws under which Divine Providence places them.

I pray that the sanctifying power of the Holy Spirit may reach the hearts of those professing Christians who have adopted the modern concept of rationalism and the postmodern concept of subjectivism. These worldviews are stealthy predators. They will do anything to garner followers. I pray they will adopt the Word of God to understand life and faith. May we all agree with the inspired words of the Psalmist:

> "Give me understanding according to Your word"

"Deliver me according to Your word"
"Teach me Your statutes"
"For all Your commandments are righteousness."
(Psalm 119:169-176)

47. Entertainment Replaces Truth

Technology, especially communications technology, popularized theological expression. In this hodge-podge of postmodern denial of truth and reality, all forms of communication technology rule. However, television was the primary tool used by postmodern theorists to promote their agenda. Is it true that "television's way of knowing is uncompromisingly hostile to typography's way of knowing?" Is it true "that television's conversations promote incoherence and triviality?" Is it true that "television speaks in only one persistent voice – the voice of entertainment?" Is it true that "television...is transforming our culture into one vast arena for show business?" Neil Postman, the author of *Amusing Ourselves to Death*, answers yes to all those questions. He concludes "it is entirely possible, of course, that in the end we shall find that delightful, and decide we like it just fine. That is exactly what Aldous Huxley feared was coming, fifty years ago."

Television was the gateway to the fun filled world of entertainment. The word "fun" is not found in Scripture. Webster defines fun as "that which provides mirth or amusement; enjoyment; playfulness." The concept or idea of entertainment is found in Scripture, but generally associated with self-indulgence by means of pagan activity (Daniel 6:18). Amusement is another word associated with evil activity (Judges 16:25). The word "play" according to Webster has 74 different nuances. One of the common uses of the word "play" is "to exercise by way of amusement or recreation." Scripture speaks often about "playing the harlot" which is an exercise of idolatry. For example when the Israelites formed the golden calf "they rose early and offered burnt offering, and brought peace offerings; and the people sat down to eat and to drink, and rose up to play (Exodus 32:6). The apostle Paul warns us not to be "idolaters, as some of them were; as it is written, "The people sat down to eat and drink, and stood up to play" (1 Corinthians 10:7). They stood up to dance around and have fun as the pagans danced before their gods.

Turn on the television and select your favorite preacher or Bible teacher. If one does not suit your individual preference, switch to another; there are hundreds available. Theological and academic credentials are no longer necessary to exegete the full counsel of God. All that is necessary is to have an "experience" with God. Diploma mills have risen to the occasion for those who want a theological degree without earning it. An uneducated, ill-equipped clergy, each generation growing exponentially with the expansion of communication technology, will result in an unhealthy church. Now handheld devices are the primary means to distribute lies and false teaching. The way to eliminate false doctrine is to, "Hold fast the pattern of sound words which you have heard from me [Paul], in faith and love which are in Christ Jesus' (2 Timothy 1:13). Then use technology to spread true doctrine.

Old Testament Israel has a notable resemblance to the New Testament Church; they are the people that belong to God. The Old Testament people of God had priests and prophets to lead in worship and teach the full counsel of God. After the death of Solomon, Jeroboam appointed himself as the leader of the people of God. What a mess! Jeroboam's unbiblical theology reminds me of cultural individualism and church autonomy. "And Jeroboam said in his heart" (1 Kings12:26), but he didn't humble himself to realize "The heart is deceitful above all things, and desperately wicked..." (Jeremiah 17:9). Since Jeroboam did not know (very likely) or simply ignored the full counsel of God, he established his own place to worship and his own idols. Then he explained to the church: "It is too much for you to go up to Jerusalem. Here are your gods, O Israel, which brought you up from the land of Egypt! And he set up one in Bethel, and the other he put in Dan. Now this thing became a sin, for the people went to worship before the one as far as Dan. He made shrines on the high places, and made priests from every class of people, who were not of the sons of Levi" (1 Kings 12:28-31).

Jeroboam interpreted or rather changed the Word of God to fit his agenda. Rather than being reformed by the Word of God, he attempted to reform the Word of God. The church followed him because he had become a celebrity among the people. A few words from that text standout as a warning to those who profess the Christian religion: [Jeroboam] "made priests from every class of people, who were not of the sons of Levi." R. L. Dabney made the comment that "Jeroboam corrupted the religion of Israel partly by making priests of the lowest of the people" (*Discussions*, vol. 2, pg.69). Communication technology may be good or bad, depending on whether the theology communicated is true or false.

Christians have deliberately and craftily established their golden calf by means of entertainment. Children are taught from birth that entertainment is necessary for their well-being. Adults are more consumed with entertainment than they are their eternal destiny. The apostle Paul warns Christians not to stand up to play. "Let him who thinks he stands take heed lest he fall" (1 Corinthians 10:12).

48. Sense, Reason, and Intellect

"In those days there was no king in Israel; everyone did what was right in his own eyes" (Judges 21:25).

Behavior that produces mass confusion is senseless. It was present in the day of the Judges and remains with us until this day. Western culture is a hotbed of various worldviews like individualism, egalitarianism, statism, pragmatism, secularism, and many more. The state is a necessary component for social and political life. However, adding "ism" to the word, "state," may indicate that the state provides the means to save the individual belonging to the state. To put it another way, statism becomes a god to worship and the way of salvation for secular life. There was a time when self-evident truths were held in high esteem in the American culture. At the same time, the church believed and taught that the Bible was absolute truth. General revelation to culture and special revelation to the church are the common threads that hold the fabric of life together. The denial of self-evident truths inclines the culture to do what is right in their own eyes. It is the denial of the inspired infallible truth of God's Word that inclines the church to agree with the culture.

This analysis of the downgrade is for western civilization in general, particularly the United States. Galileo wisely observed, "I do not feel obliged to believe that the same God who has endowed us with sense, reason, and intellect has intended us to forgo their use." Muse that quote from Galileo about "sense, reason, and intellect." Then ponder the misuse, abuse, and absconding of those three disciplines to discover the reason this country is in such a mess. The scholar (one schooled or taught a particular doctrine) has replaced the intellect (one who uses the rational powers naturally endowed and applies rationality by the use of a tool known as logic). For example, Barak Obama is said to be a scholar and he may be, but he is no intellect. The scholars who argued against Galileo's heliocentric views were so blind in the field of astronomy, but so schooled in theology, failed to use their natural "sense, reason, and intellect."

I'll make two comments about the current political problems. The two comments may be summarized within two political philosophies: Statism and sophism.

Statism is the political worldview of the liberal political machine. Statism basically says the state is the savior of its subjects. Or to put it another way the government will solve all your problems. Just turn over your mind and the minds of your children to me (big brother) and turn over your money and your children's money to the state and they will solve all your problems. The goal of the liberal political machine is a national lobotomy.

Sophism is the art and use of empty words in the context of a subtle false argument to convince someone that what is false is true. Let me quote Clement of Alexandria on the subject of sophistry.

> The art of sophistry, which the Greeks cultivated, is a fantastic power, which makes false opinions like true by means of words. For it produces rhetoric in order to persuasion, and disputation for wrangling. These arts, therefore, if not conjoined with philosophy, will be injurious to everyone. For Plato openly called sophistry "an evil art." And Aristotle, following him, demonstrates it to be a dishonest art, which abstracts in a specious manner the whole business of wisdom, and professes a wisdom which it has not studied. (*Clement's Stromata*, chap. 8)

Sophistry drives statism or any other false worldview by means of the belligerent person using the tools to win his or her agenda.

Postmodern adherents employ sophisticated tactics to demean logic, reason, sense and intellect. The segments of society that have abandoned those God given sources are the ones that elect ungodly, unreasonable, anti-intellectual politicians. They have hoodwinked nearly half of the voting democracy. They use the power of sophism and the charm of statism to gain power and wealth.

If you're like me, 70 or over, we will probably not live long enough to see a serious collapse. However your children, grandchildren and the generations that follow will suffer unless someone discovers or rediscovers the root of the problem and will courageously address it publicly.

The root of the problem is "we" (collectively) have to admit that we've been duped by the various political powers at each level of government during each administration in recent history. Slowly but surely each generation was trapped by the idea that the State could better manage the affairs of life than private citizens. Once we (collectively) admit our complacency, we must act collectively to restore our nation incrementally to a level of constitutional integrity.

The "Tea Party" concept was one way to prevent the devolution of our sad estate unto the coming generation. Individuals and groups collectively should organize to educate the public that contemporary scholarship is an anti-intellectual educational philosophy and restore Galileo's Trio: sense, reason, and intellect. The church should seek reformation so it may be a cultural change agent to the glory of God.

49. Image Is Not Everything

A few years ago Neil Postman wrote a book entitled *Amusing Ourselves to Death*. Mr. Postman examined the deep and broad effects of television culture and how "entertainment values" have corrupted the way we think. It is the fast moving imagery on television and the movie theater that entertains and amuses the human senses. The public square has posited the notion that image is everything and rational discourse in the public arena has been absconded by the neo-aesthetic postmodern culture. The academy has lost its zeal for a rational moral philosophy or an informed theology to address the public square.

Mr. Postman's thesis is "to show that a great media-metaphor shift has taken place in America, with the result that the content of much of our public discourse has become dangerous nonsense." Everything from politics to religion has been affected by the image media (TV, computers, cell phones, etc.).

Mr. Postman's book cites examples of how Christianity has shifted from theology to show business. To put Mr. Postman's illustrations in context, his book was written in 1985. Mr. Postman used the following illustration to make his point. "Not long ago, I saw Billy Graham join with Shecky Green, Red Buttons, Dionne Warwick, Milton Berle and other theologians in a tribute to George Burns, who was celebrating himself for surviving eighty years in show business. The Reverend Graham exchanged one-liners with Burns about making preparations for Eternity. Although the Bible makes no mention of it, the Reverend Graham assured the audience that God loves those who make people laugh. It was an honest mistake. He merely mistook NBC for God."

The sad news is that amusement has become the popular method of ministry even among those who call themselves Bible believing evangelicals. The emerging modernity of the 20th century fed the flames of the church growth movement so that amusement became a way of life for the ministry of the church. Mr. Postman made two observations after watching 42 hours of religious programs (i.e.

Robert Schuller, Jimmy Swaggart, Jim Bakker, Pat Robertson, and others). His first observation was "that on television, religion, like everything else, is presented quite simply and without apology, as entertainment. Everything that makes religion an historic, profound and sacred human activity is stripped away; there is no ritual, no dogma, no tradition, no theology, and above all no sense of spiritual transcendence. On these shows, the preacher is tops. God comes out as second banana." His second observation was that the TV preachers do not have the education, theological acumen, and expositional skills of pastor's and theologians of previous generations.

Sometimes I find myself amused at the tragedy of this headlong leap into disaster, but my amusement quickly turns into contemplative musing. There is a radical difference between the terms amuse and muse. Amusement comes from the word amuse. Most people think of the word amuse in terms of entertainment, most often with a comical aspect. "He is so amusing" meaning his entertainment is funny. The word "muse" refers to meditation and most often a state of profound meditation. I hope God will be pleased to save His church from amusing itself to death.

I recommend Neil Postman's *Amusing Ourselves to Death*. It has an appropriate sub-title, *Public Discourse in the Age of Show Business*.

50. Is the Debate Table Closed?

A nationally known and respected preacher made some blunders referring to Jonathan Edwards. His statements could lead people to believe that Jonathan Edwards was not a Calvinist. I had read enough of Edwards to know that the preacher was wrong and I wrote and told him that he was wrong. I liked the preacher then, I still like the preacher, and he has some good things to say relative to biblical doctrine. After sharing this incident with a fellow minister he said, "Martin, you shouldn't be so hard on Rev. T. V. Preacher." My statement was true; his was false and, in fact, I may have saved the preacher from further embarrassment. In some sense, all ministers have the responsibility to warn other ministers about making haphazard statements contrary to the Word of God. It certainly is dangerous for the church to lose the desire for truth. God told Ezekiel, "I have appointed you a watchman to the house of Israel; whenever you hear a word from My mouth, warn them from Me" (Ezekiel 3:17).

There are times when we get offended without thinking through a statement or proposition. Make sure you understand words and how the words are used in the context. Remember, there are two different kinds of opinions. There is the orthodox view, which is the right opinion or proper opinion as set forth by some authority. The other kind of opinion is known as a heresy. The word heresy comes from the Greek word *hairesis* that denotes a choice that leads to factions or divisions. It is, or should be, the goal of all Christians to be orthodox.

I remember working with a small group in Central Florida to start a church and one man in the group was a prominent person in the community. My first impression was that he was a normal, intelligent, thinking man. Over the course of a few months I realized that truth was relative to his mind. One night after a long discussion about truth he said, "How do you know you are right and the Roman Catholic Church is wrong?" After presenting a rational, cogent defense, I realized he rejected intelligent, logical, and reasonable language. Rationality was not in his vocabulary. Such abandonment of rational thinking will ultimately destroy orthodoxy and introduce heresy of every sort.

It could be that I spent too many years as a pagan and I just expect too much out of Christianity. When there are contradictions and heresies, Christians must defend the truth from the full counsel of God. There are times when I expose contradictions and heresies. Sometimes it seems like a vicious circle with a guilt complex on one side and a burning burden for truth on the other side.

The Book of Psalms was given to Christians, because through it God touches our emotions, affections, heart, viscera or simply put the innermost being. In the Psalms we find repeated reference to God's truth, as a matter of fact, the word truth is used more times in the Book of Psalms than any other book of the Bible. I don't have the monopoly on truth, but neither is my mind a *tabla rasa* (blank slate). The truth is that two very fine professors, R. C. Sproul and John Gerstner, taught me to be careful, thorough, systematic, and precise as a theologian.

I believe we should be at the table discussing the theological issues that separate us. The effort is worthy of our prayers. No is my response to popular polls as the method for determining truth. It is not likely that Christians will come to a fuller understanding of the nature and character of God by conducting popular opinion polls. The giants of the Christian Church have always used intelligent discourse at the debate table, the apostle Paul being at the forefront to glorify God.

51. Postmodern Culture Accommodates the Church

In a popular academic work by Steven Conner there is a quote by Michael Ryan, a postmodern liberal. He said:

> Rather than being expressive representations of a substance taken to be prior, cultural signs become instead active agents in themselves, creating new substances, new social forms, new ways of acting and thinking, new attitudes, reshuffling the cards of 'fate' and 'nature' and social 'reality'. It is on this margin that culture, seemingly entirely autonomous and detached, turns around and becomes a social and material force, a power of signification that discredits all claims to substantive grounds outside representation and this discrediting applies to political institutions, moral norms, social practices and economic structure. (*Postmodernist culture*, p. 225)

The postmodern culture has pronounced the death sentence on absolute truth and reality; therefore, according to the postmodern agenda we have to reshuffle the cards of fate, nature, and reality. The deck of cards according to the postmodern agenda plays out this way; political institutions, moral norms, social practices, and economic structures are signified by our culture and expressed by representatives of that culture. Alasdair MacIntyre, in his book, *After Virtue*, identified the cultural representatives in three categories. They are the manager, therapist, and aesthete. They represent the cultural elites and everyone follows their lead. Managers have authority in public life, therapists have influence in personal life and the aesthete resonates with alleged beauty in modern media. These cultural representatives are modern sophists. Their social engineering is deceptive at the root.

The expressions of our cultural dilemma are noticed when it used to be that we heard of adults committing suicide, but now that is a common practice among teenagers. Saving owls is more important than saving babies. Where will it all end?

In the postmodern culture, words are meaningless. Therefore, a preacher, politician, or professor can tell a lie and "it's all good." The church has been seduced by Satan's lies. Now, the postmodern culture charms professing Christians with deceptive statements like, "absolute objective truth is not necessary for cultural civility." According to Richard Tarnas, the postmodernist states, "the nature of truth and reality, in science no less than in philosophy, religion, or art, is radically ambiguous" (*The Passion of the Western Mind*, by Richard Tarnas, p. 397). The church stands silent in the midst of an ever-darkening culture.

Dr. Os Guinness in his book, *Time For Truth*, observes that "in a postmodern world, the question is not 'Is it true?' but rather 'Whose truth is it?' and 'Which power stands to gain?'" If you do not understand postmodern theory, it is like cancer. It is silent, ever present, poisonous, and possesses stealthy metastasis qualities. To put it another way, postmodern theory is killing the evangelical church in the US and the western Judeo-Christian ethic.

Postmodernism fertilizes the culture with ungodly worldviews while church leaders idly stand by and observe the cultural battles. Let me quote from, *The Dominant Culture*:

> The church in every generation tends to accommodate the culture rather than being an instrument of reformation for culture. Any ungodly culture will try to change the church into a more accommodating organization. How is this accomplished? The culture says to the professing Christian, "follow me and you will be like God." Every generation becomes raptured into a state of ecstasy and falls into the trap of cultural accommodation. The church becomes enslaved by the ideas and fashions of men; the culture devours the church as a beast devours its prey. An example of being "raptured into a state of ecstasy," is the shift from the pastor being a shepherd for the congregation (Acts 20:28) to the pastor who is like a chief executive officer of a corporation. The culture has convinced the church that bureaucratic mangers are more important that godly elders watching over the flock. The

church has followed the culture with psychological manipulations to sooth the heartache of a sinful soul. The manipulative ideas of an ungodly culture are charming and appealing, unless the Word of God is held forth as the ultimate means to determine the doctrine and practice of the church.

52. Terrorism Strikes Again

The terror of terrorism is natural to the human race after sin entered the world. The terror that struck a small Christian congregation in Texas caused frenzy among the media, law enforcement and the general public. The event and the man who murdered and maimed the majority of the congregation has everyone befuddled. Looking for the reason of this murderous event, it has been called "evil against good" while many are blaming it on "mental illness." Those terms belong to theologically ignorant people.

The question on the tip of the tongue is, "what causes terrorism?" The answer is the *noetic* effect of sin. Man's sinfulness was demonstrated when a man walked in a building and started killing people at random. The human race is sinful and the only remedy is for God to change the hearts of sinful men so they will believe the truth and claims of Jesus Christ and trust Him for salvation and eternal life.

It is not possible to discover spiritual truth by psychological inquiry. Sin is a spiritual issue (metaphysical mind) not a psychological issue (physical brain). I begin by asking the question, "What is Sin." Sin is the lack of absolute righteousness and failure to perfectly keep all of God's commandments. Total depravity is a concept that explains the biblical doctrine of sin. The word depravity refers to corruption, so sin refers to the total corruption of man, both body and soul. Total depravity is an appropriate concept because it brings the totality of human nature into the picture. It raises the question: Is human nature good or evil? Do people sin because they are sinners by nature or do they sin because of their social and environmental circumstances? The Bible answers the question: "Surely I was sinful at birth, sinful from the time my mother conceived me" (Psalm 51:5). Are people basically good? The answer is no. The Bible explains: "He was setting out on a journey, a man ran up to Him and knelt before Him, and asked Him, "Good Teacher, what shall I do to inherit eternal life?" And Jesus said to him, "Why do you call Me good? No one is good except God alone" (Mark

10:17-18). The effect of sin will shine like the sun if we consult the Word of God.

The Greek word *nous* essentially refers to the mind, reason, or understanding. The word *noetic* comes from the Greek word *nous*. The *noetic* effect of sin refers to the mind, so the question must be asked: to what extent did the fall of man affect the mind? The *noetic* structure (the function of the mind) refers to the sum total of everything a person knows and consequently believes. For instance, Adam's ability to reason before the Fall was like the rest of creation; it was perfect. The *noetic* effect of sin did not destroy reason, but rather defaced it.

In Christian theology, this is the metaphysical aspect of the soul that is the center of reason, intelligence, and understanding. The mind of God is perfect unlike the mind of sinful man. The Bible uses the Greek word *nous* to describe the condition of humanity without God (Romans 1:28). The Bible also uses a word connected with *nous* to describe the human ability to understand God by the power of the mind (Romans 1:20). The physical brain will cease to exist, but the mind will remain forever (*Theological Terms in Layman Language,* by Martin Murphy, p. 72)

Other than a few isolated cases of a malfunctioning brain such as chemical imbalances, which may result in murder, terrorism is an evil way of life that ends with murder. Biblical and natural law prohibits murder, without a cause. Some people are deceived by the outward personality and words of a terrorist. They may appear peaceable for years before their evil character emerges. "Woe to those who devise iniquity, and work out evil on their beds! At morning light they practice it, because it is in the power of their hand" (Micah 2:1).

The prophet Jeremiah explains the natural condition of the human race. "The heart is deceitful above all things, and desperately wicked; Who can know it" (Jeremiah 17:9)? The sin nature is the underlying cause of all sin and terrorism is sin.

53. What Does Your World Look Like?

In your community, town, state, and nation, there are embedded worldviews. A worldview helps you identify the way you understand life. Principles, good or bad, build and express your worldviews. Dr. J. P. Moreland explains the nature of a worldview:

> A person's worldview contains two important features. First, it includes the set of beliefs the person accepts, especially those about important matters such as reality, God, value, knowledge, and so on…[and] a worldview includes the rational structure that occurs among the set of beliefs that constitute it. (*Kingdom Triangle*, by J. P. Moreland, p. 33)

Worldviews are formed and confirmed by the way a person interprets the world around him or her. Christian worldviews derive from truth, because God is truth. Ungodly and unbiblical worldviews are derived from falsehood (lies) articulated by Satan, the father of lies. It only takes one step to turn a legitimate discipline in life, like being human into a worldview, which then turns into a false god. To put it another way worldviews may become objects of worship.

The easy way to identify and express worldviews is the "ism" attached to the end of a noun. When the noun forming suffix, "ism," is added to the end of a noun, it describes an ideology or a way of life. Christians should have some knowledge of how the various "isms" affect them corporately as a church and individually as Christians. It is the duty of Christians to formulate a worldview that places the God they worship in the centerpiece of their thinking. It is a way of life that has ultimate value for you, your community, your town, or your nation. When the majority assume a worldview, it is "the dominant worldview." The following worldviews are mere samples of many used in modern/postmodern culture.

> <u>Theism</u> is the fundamental worldview of the Christian religion. Theism is the worldview that acknowledges our

relationship to God in a personal way and further that God's nature and character is what is claimed in the Word of God.

Humanism is contrary to theism. A brief description of humanism: "Humanism asserts that the nature of the universe depicted by modern science makes unacceptable any supernatural or cosmic guarantees of human values" (American Humanist Association). An ancient Greek philosopher named Protagoras has given the modern humanist a motto: "Man, the measure." Protagoras believed that man was the measure of all things.

Secularism is the most misinterpreted worldview. The root of the word Secularism is derived from the word secular. The word secular describes the here and now. Secular is actually a good word because we all live in the here and now. However, when you turn it into a worldview it means, "Live for today, because there may not be a tomorrow." Secularism is probably the most influential worldview and is in direct opposition to theism. Theism places the importance on the sacred rather than the secular, the divine rather than the human, the truth rather than expedience, and the good life rather than the happy life.

Naturalism is the worldview that denies the existence of a theistic God. Naturalism believes the Universe is natural and energy and matter is the substance of existence. Naturalism denies the spiritual nature of man. Humanism, secularism, and naturalism are contrary to theism and supernaturalism.

Individualism is the worldview that produces irresponsible and mass confusion in the church and in the culture. An individual person is a creative work of God. However, when the noun forming suffix, "ism," is added to the word "individual," it describes an ideology or a way of life. Individualism may become a false god to the individual. The philosophy of individualism places self at the center of life. "I am and there is no one else besides me" (Isaiah 47:10).

Statism is the worldview that gives the state all sovereignty and authority over its "collective equals." Webster defines it as "the principle or policy of concentrating extensive economic, political, and related controls in the state at the cost of individual liberty." The state then becomes the savior of those collective equals. Statism recruits egalitarianism as an accompanying worldview. Egalitarianism is the worldview that claims all people are equal. Allan Bloom in his book, The *Closing of the American Mind*, reasons that, "Although every man in a democracy thinks himself individually the equal of every other man, this makes it difficult to resist the collectivity of equal men." This however, is another danger in our American system of government. The result of two centuries of American democratic federalism has produced the statism of our present day. This is one of the most influential worldviews in the United States.

Victimizationalism is a passive worldview that was popularized by an unbiblical therapeutic generation accompanied by a litigious society. It is a worldview void of any biblical understanding. The basic assumption behind victimizationalism is the goodness and worth of self. It is built on the unbiblical notion that "I am and there is not one else besides me" (Isaiah 47:10). This unbiblical destructive worldview essentially says, "When something bad happens to me it is the fault of someone else. On a practical level the alleged victim says, "Since it is their fault, they must pay me some money."

Feminism was born at the feet of egalitarianism, individualism, and statism. The fundamental ideology is that women have equal rights, the same rights that men have as a secular worldview. If taken to its logical end, it would mean that women desire to dominate men. Now, where did that come from? Maybe from the mouth of God! "To the woman he [God] said, 'I will greatly increase your labor pains; with pain you will give birth to children. You will want to control your husband, but he will dominate you'" (Genesis 3:16). As punishment for breaking God's covenant, Eve the woman would desire to control Adam the man. It has been part of the old man (sinful nature) since the beginning.

There are many more worldviews, but the real question is, which will you choose? There are plenty of ungodly worldviews like pragmatism, consumerism, sophism, deism, hedonism, narcissism, relativism, utilitarianism, and multiculturalism; Just to mention a few of the most popular false gods. Three letters, "ism," may lead a professing Christian down a destructive path. Look and listen for "isms" then do a little research and study the whole counsel of God because, there you will find the truth.

54. Sophism is Stealthy Deception

This morning I listened to some of the congressional hearings relative to Russia's influence on the elections and alleged wire-tapping by the Obama administration. This is utterly unimportant compared to the North Korea Nuclear threats. However, when I listen to someone speak, unless it is casual conversation, I listen for rational, intelligent, logical words expressed by ultimate principles. When the spokesman for the Democratic Party started talking I immediately thought of Tertullus and the worldview known as sophism. Let me explain.

The distance between truth and falsehood is not very far, if reality is not important. In early Greek philosophy, sophism was a worldview that employed specious arguments to deceive someone. Sophism was the basis for deception; stealth was the practice of sophism. Paul the apostle was trained to defend the truth against stealthy deception. The pursuit of truth was considered a virtue in Paul's worldview. However, at the beginning of the 21st century, poll after poll indicates that if there is any truth, it does not matter. Perhaps the stealthy deception of sophism is the reason why so many Christian leaders convincingly get away with not telling the truth. Parents admonish their children to tell the truth, but adults laugh at little white lies. The enemy of truth in any generation is the evil art of sophistry. The first Christian scholar was probably Clement of Alexandria. Although little is known of his life, he was one of the early defenders of the Christian religion. In one of his writings he explained the principle of sophism.

Sophistry is a subtle false argument. To sophisticate means to mislead by deception and false arguments. To be sophisticated is actually bad, although a revised contemporary meaning is that a sophisticated person is worldly wise, mature, classy, in the know, and on top of all situations. If the root word "sophism" is an enemy to truth, how can its derivative word "sophisticated" be good for truth? For instance, worldly wise does not necessarily express truth.

The history of Christianity reveals the presence of sophism in every generation. In the 16th century, John Calvin said:

The argument against Christianity unfolds itself and discloses the tangled web of their sophistries, men of discernment see at once that what they have apprehended is nothing at all. I see that the world everywhere trifles with God, and that the ungodly delude themselves with Sophistries. (*Calvin's Commentary on Nahum*)

The 19th century Presbyterian theologian, James H. Thornwell said, "The sophist of speculation is the hypocrite." Sophism and stealthy deception always has and always will be an enemy to the church for every generation and all cultures.

In the text of Acts 24 and 25, Paul makes his defense before Felix the governor of Judea. The Jews from Jerusalem came to charge Paul with the hope that Felix would turn Paul over to them or better yet that Felix would have Paul put to death. The Jewish leaders from Jerusalem brought a spokesman with them. His name was Tertullus. Whether he was a Jew or Roman lawyer is speculative. He appears to have been knowledgeable with Roman law and has a Roman name. Felix the governor called on Tertullus to state his case.

In the typical style of that day, Tertullus should acknowledge the governor's office and authority. Tertullus addressed the governor and accredited Felix with bringing peace and prosperity to Judea. That was a lie, a big lie. Felix brought trouble, dissension, suspension, and terror to that part of the Middle East. Then Tertullus said Felix was a man of foresight. That was a lie. Family connections and intrigue got him the position. His corruption caused so much trouble that Nero finally recalled Felix. Tertullus skillfully lied, as any sophist does, to gain favor with the governor.

Tertullus eventually said there were three charges against Paul. First, Paul was charged with being a troublemaker. In the New King James Version, the phrase "creator of dissension" derives from a Greek word that is related to the English word "plague." The sophisticated and stealthy charge is that Paul's doctrine was like an infectious disease. It would spread throughout the empire. It was alleged that Paul's doctrine was a real danger for the Roman Empire. Second, Paul was charged with being a ringleader of the sect of the Nazarenes. A ringleader is always considered a threat by the state. Third, Tertullus said Paul tried to desecrate the Temple. Of the three charges, this is the only one of significance. Rome had given the Jews permission to impose the death penalty to anyone who defiled the temple. All three charges were merely accusations. However, they were very effectively presented by way of sophistry and deceptive stealth.

Tertullus stated these points as if they were true and ultimately deserved condemnation. Tertullus concluded his arguments with an agreement from the Jews present. He told Felix, "by examining him yourself you may ascertain all these things of which we accuse him." Tertullus assumed that his deception and cunning was believable. Felix should believe the charges because Tertullus made them, the Jews present for the trial agreed and the democracy, that is the mob at Jerusalem, had voted against Paul.

There was no place for truth, but the sophist forgot a fundamental axiom. Truth is always true even if nobody believes it. Falsehood is false even if everybody believes it. Os Guinness has rightly said, "Without truth we are all vulnerable to manipulation."

Paul's defense before Felix was radically and truthfully different from the deceptive rhetoric of Tertullus. Paul clearly stated that he was not a troublemaker. He was only in Jerusalem for six days. He did not even preach while he was there. Paul disputed no one while he was there. He did not even gather a crowd of people except the democracy without a conscience.

Paul admitted he was a follower of the way, but certainly not a ringleader. Anyhow, Roman law allowed Paul to practice his religion just as it allowed the Jews to practice their religion. Paul's final defense was, "I did not desecrate the temple." In fact, Paul was submitting to the Jewish law and was ceremonially clean. There was no sophistry in Paul's defense. There was no stealthy deception. There was no wrangling with words. Truth was Paul's only defense. A nation that gives in to the deception of sophistry by stealth will lose the freedom to tell the truth.

55. Feminism in the American Culture

The prevalent feminism in the American culture has produced two undesirable effects.

> 1. Satan used a sinful secular doctrine (Jacobin egalitarianism – the political party during the French Revolution positing absolute/perfect equality) so the biblical doctrine of familial and marital covenants appear to be old fashioned. Since the fall of the human race, the female desires to rule over the male. A woman may desire to serve as a preacher in the church or a president of a nation, but it is a sinful desire. I will be redundant for the purpose of emphasis: "To the woman he [God] said, 'I will greatly increase your labor pains; with pain you will give birth to children. You will want to control your husband, but he will dominate you'" (Genesis 3:16). God's plan was for order and harmony, not equality and strife.

> 2. It creates a dysfunctional family. It opens Pandora's Box for the woman to vote for her candidate of choice and the man to vote for the candidate of his choice, which neutralizes political theory in the home. It leaves the children with an example of ungodly and unbiblical leadership in the home.

The state should follow a simple biblical principle. Christians have an ultimate authority that will prevent these undesirable effects of feminization. "Wives submit to your own husbands, as to the Lord" (Ephesians 5:22). This verse is not a reference to blind and blanket submission. However, no submission leads to anarchy and absolute submission leads to tyranny. Although anarchy and tyranny are present, to a greater or lesser degree in many marriages, the doctrine of submission usually falls under one of three categories.

- Patriarchy refers to the husband is the head of the family.
- Matriarchy refers to the wife is head of the family.

- Democracy refers to no rule of the family, therefore anarchy prevails in the family.

The enemies of submission are:

> 1) Self-centeredness – A person who is governed by the thought that everything revolves around him or her.
> 2) Dictatorial arrogance – Another aspect of the self by lording it over others. The dictator wants absolute control.
> 3) Individualism – The world view that displaces the confederation concept. The Bible describes individualism in terms of, "I am and there is no one else besides me" (Isaiah 47:10). Individualism literally says, "My opinions are the ones that count and if I can't have it my way I will not play in the game."
> 4) Thoughtlessness – One who is unconcerned with respect to the needs, desires and welfare of others.
> 5) Self-seeking – One who is interested in the outcome only for the benefit of self.

The 19th century theologian, Dr. Robert L. Dabney put it in these terms and I shall quote so as not to add or take away from these most profound words. Dabney said: "the wife must obey the husband in the sense of conceding to him the final decision of joint domestic questions, within the bound of her higher duty to God and conscience or the husband must obey the wife, or the marriage is virtually annulled" (*Practical Philosophy* p. 367). Please notice two important points:

> 1) Obey the husband within the bounds of her higher duty to God and conscience. (Obey God rather than man.)
> 2) If she does not obey her husband (unless he has told her to think or act in a way that is unbiblical or ungodly) the marriage is virtually annulled.

If there is no submission there is no marriage. One word will sum up the role of the wife in marriage – submit.

Likewise, one word will sum up the role of the husband in marriage – love.

A marriage does not exist if the husband does not love his wife just as Christ loved the church and gave Himself for her.

The husband must be willing to sacrifice everything for his wife. It is the duty of the husband to love his wife so he may be the instrument for the sanctification of his wife.

The word love is not merely a reference to sensual and friendly love. The husband has a distinctive love for his wife. It's called Christian love. It is the kind of love that is sacrificial, so that whether it is a love in confrontation or a love in encouragement, it is a godly love.

Since the church is in a state of disorder and lacks a proper understanding of God's prescribed order for submission and love in the marriage, the culture and political life follows suit.

The mandate for Christians is simple. Submit yourself to the Word of God and pray for the Spirit of God to enlighten your mind, to incline your will and motivate your emotions so you will find harmony and order in your marriage relationship. It will have a positive and meaningful effect on the political life of the nation.

56. Victimizationalism

The headline in the local newspaper was "State Department of Education will go after BP" (British Petroleum) to recover revenues because of the oil spill. The rationale was state sales tax will be down because of the oil spill and therefore the school system will have less revenue. The irony is that the education budget is a perpetual problem.

The top shelf at the education department ought to exercise themselves so they may discover the reason for budget shortfalls. If they were honest, they would discover the problem is not merely the oil spill in the Gulf of Mexico. The reason for their budget shortfalls are abuses and unnecessary programs within the school system.

The real problem is the world and life view owned by the accusers. One of the more popular milieus is victimizationalism. This is a passive world view that was popularized by the therapeutic generation accompanied by a litigious society. It is a world view void of any biblical understanding. However, it is as old as the human race. It all began a long time ago when the first human being was instructed not to do something [the tree of the knowledge of good and evil you shall not eat] (Genesis 2:17). Humans will be humans! They think they know more than God knows and they think they know what is best. Characterized by, "I know what the Word of God says, but..." so Adam ate from the forbidden tree. God asked Adam, "have you eaten from the tree?" Adam, the first alleged victim, blamed it on Eve (Genesis 3:12). Adam implies that it is God's fault because God gave Adam the woman; Adam didn't ask for her. The victim blames everyone else, but the Bible makes a clear declaration: "But each one is tempted when he drawn away by his own desires and enticed (James 1:14). In his book, *After Virtue*, Alasdair MacIntyre asserts that, "Philip Rieff has documented with devastating insight a number of the ways in which truth has been displaced as a value and replaced by psychological effectiveness." MacIntyre further asserts, "The idioms of therapy have invaded all too successfully such spheres as those of education and of religion." Lawyers love victimizationalism and the rest of society just doesn't give a tinkers mound.

The basic assumption behind victimizationalism is the goodness and worth of self. It is built on the unbiblical notion that "I am and there is not one else besides me" (Isaiah 47:10). This unbiblical destructive world view essentially says "when something bad happens to me it is the fault of someone else. Since it is their fault, they must pay me some money.

Now Christians, let's hear the rest of the story. The Bible says "each one is tempted when he is drawn away by his own desires and enticed. Then, when desire has conceived, it gives birth to sin..." (James 1:14, 15). The sin nature always puts the blame on someone else just like Eve said, "the Devil made me do it" (Genesis 3:8-13). The unbiblical therapeutic enterprise attempts to avoid the sin problem and dwell on the goodness of man. They would do well to dwell on the goodness of God and the badness of man.

57. Consumerism: The Worldview That Makes People Happy

A friend was very excited to find out that I had become a Christian. I remember him saying "you're still a salesman, you've just switched products." He was aware that I was once in the sales field. Out of my ignorance, I agreed with him, but I now realize that God is not for sell at any price or under any conditions.

The fundamental goal for most Americans is to be "happy." All of life is shaped around the desire to be self-fulfilled and happy. The French Revolution certainly had a profound influence on the concept of "happiness." Liberty, equality, and fraternity became the watch words that would bring the desired happiness to every successive generation. Do you want to be happy? The worldview known as consumerism suggests that happiness comes from instant gratification. "Things" will bring happiness.

This is not just a philosophical worldview. Selling Jesus Christ has become an art among many evangelical Christians. Evangelism is no longer God-centered, but rather it is consumer-centered. Even more significant is the loss of God-centered worship and especially God-centered preaching. When you go to worship next Sunday pay particular attention to the worship service. You may find there is more of a focus on entertainment, than on the infinite, eternal, all powerful, all knowing and ever present God whose character is marked by "wisdom, holiness, justice, goodness and truth." All of these significant characteristics of God take a casual part in many worship services, if they are mentioned at all. Singers try to dazzle the audience with their sensational music. Preachers preach to "felt needs" using popular aphorisms, rarely expounding from the Word of God or using sound exegetical and hermeneutical skills. In short, entertainment is creating havoc within evangelical Christianity. Erich Fromm once said, "Modern man, if he dared to be articulate about his concept of heaven, would describe a vision which would look like the biggest department store in the world."

Dr. David Wells has rightly observed.

Malls are monuments to consumption – but so are mega-churches. Both places celebrate the coupling of the appetites of consumption with religion. The religion of the mall has been condensed into the secular creed that "to have is to be;" in the mega-church, the psychological need to consume is expressed as a form of spiritual hunger, a need to be connected with others.

The entertainment industry is the fodder that feeds the starving consumer. Advertiser's pay the entertainer to perform in such a way that will compel the consumer to buy a little bit of happiness. Television, radio, and social media are the gateway to the fun filled world of entertainment. The word "fun" is not found in Scripture. Webster defines fun as "that which provides mirth or amusement; enjoyment; playfulness." The concept or idea of entertainment is found in Scripture, but generally associated with self-indulgence by means of pagan activity (Daniel 6:18). Amusement is another word associated with evil activity (Judges 16:25). The word "play", according to Webster, has 74 different nuances. One of the common uses of the word "play" is "to exercise by way of amusement or recreation." Scripture speaks often about "playing the harlot" which is an exercise of idolatry. For example when the Israelites formed the golden calf "they rose early and offered burnt offering, and brought peace offerings; and the people sat down to eat and to drink, and rose up to play (Exodus 32:6). The apostle Paul warns us not to be "idolaters, as some of them were; as it is written, "The people sat down to eat and drink, and stood up to play" (1 Corinthians 10:7). They stood up to dance around and have fun as the pagans danced before their gods.

The church should be reminded from Holy Scripture: "You say, 'I am rich; I have acquired wealth and do not need a thing.' But you do not realize that you are wretched, pitiful, poor, blind and naked" (Revelation 3:17).

Christians trust the creative and providential hand of the all-powerful God. They receive and rest upon Christ alone for salvation and gain assurance of the power of the Holy Spirit in their lives. Christians ought to delight in consuming Christ and the spiritual feast He provides for the children of God.

58. Pragmatism: The Worldview That Works

When a fast food restaurant considers the possibility of opening a new location they first examine the demographics. They want to know how many vehicles pass by the location each day, trends in population growth and much more statistical data. Why? They want it to be successful. They want the business to work.

Pragmatism is the world view that states: "if it works it must be right." The Greek word *pragma* from which we get the word "pragmatic" basically means to execute or to carry out some deed or task. At the end of 20th century that meaning has been distorted by other worldviews and now the emphasis is on practicality and expediency.

Is there anything wrong with being practical? No, absolutely not! However, as a worldview, pragmatism is often in conflict with Christianity. I have often heard and used the phrase "where there is a will there is a way." Pragmatism is the dynamic worldview expressed in that statement. While I am writing this article, a robbery is occurring someplace in this nation. The person committing the criminal act simply wills to rob another person and therefore pragmatically accomplishes the crime. It is never right to do wrong no matter how good the results may seem.

Pastors often tell me that "such and such" works for them. This is particularly applied to the doctrine of worship, ranging from traditional to contemporary. However, God is not pragmatic on the doctrine. God's displeasure towards false worship does not have a good ending. Christians ought to read the account of false worship in Leviticus chapter ten. The Lord gave specific instructions for offering worship relative to the use of fire and incense (Leviticus 16:12). It is clear that God commanded Nadab and Abihu, the worship leaders, to worship a specific way and they offered worship "which He [God] had not commanded them" (Leviticus 10:1-2). Nabad and Abihu were punished most severely for their pragmatic approach to worship.

The desire to be practical has been and continues to be a detriment to the spiritual well-being of the church. Pragmatism leads to the spiritual illness, which is widespread in the 20th century evangelical church.

The ultimate danger with pragmatism is its relationship to humanism and secularism.

In his book *Made in America* Mike Horton points out that "a casual inventory of evangelical periodicals, tapes, and books reveals that there is little difference between the Christian's demand for a utilitarian faith and non-Christian's never-ending search for a new fix." Humanism looks to man for truth. Secularism looks to this present world to find truth. Pragmatism is a technique of the humanist/secularist to replace truth.

How should the church respond? The same way Jesus responded to Satan when Satan tempted Jesus with all the kingdoms of this world. Jesus responded "Away from me, Satan! For it is written... ." Jesus did not respond with a pragmatic answer. Jesus responded by citing the Word of God as the eternal truth and that eternal truth is the only response and action that a Christian may follow.

59. Education: The Great Human Challenge

Any philosophy of education will include a God-centered world and life view. Democratic idealism, enlightenment thinking, natural rights theory or any worldview that denigrates reason is an enemy of true education. Reason is "God's gift to the human race that gives humans the ability to think rationally, and therefore intelligently. Reason is the ground of intellectual ability and the seat of all knowledge" (*Theological Terms*, p. 111). The English word "reason" derives from the Latin word *ratio* that employs the laws of logic to construct a theory for knowledge. Reasoning defined by the *Dictionary of Philosophy* is the, "Faculty of connecting ideas consciously, and purposively. Thinking in logical form." Reasonable logic demands an effect from a sufficient cause. My question for this discussion is, "if atheism is the effect, what is the non-theistic cause?" Reasoning went aghast! Where is the apostle Paul? "And he entered the synagogue and continued speaking out boldly for three months, reasoning and persuading them about the Kingdom of God." The atheists see little reasoning from the church. Then Paul went to the Reason Rally or to use the biblical terminology Paul "took away the disciples, reasoning daily in the school of Tyrannus." (Acts 19:8-9).

Education must be defined for any progress in this discussion. The word "education" is often used to describe the general process of passing information to others. To put it another way, education has become a generic term, concept, and philosophy used by people who have an agenda for passing along, sometimes objective, but primarily subjective ideas. There are two Greek words that are translated educate and used during the development of western civilization. *Paideuo*, although translated educate primarily referred to the process of training children. Sometimes the word *paideuo* was translated discipline, which naturally accompanies training. The concept of training a child fits the description of a school or the university. The school is the place where a teacher gives information to a scholar. The scholar learns, *paideuo*, from the teacher. Therefore, it may be said that education is that process whereby a teacher passes along information to a student who may be subject to discipline if the student ignores the instruction. The result would be that the student would have enough information to carry out certain duties in life.

Another Greek word *manthano* is also translated "to educate." The Greek word *manthano* may be traced to another Greek word *math* from which we get the English word "mathematics." Plato used this word to refer to "the mathematical sciences, especially arithmetic, geometry, and astronomy." It was used by Greek philosophers such as Parmenides, 475 B.C., through the New Testament era into the first century. It primarily, but not exclusively, referred to the process of learning by study. It appears that the early Greek thinkers associated the word *manthano* with rational, logical, and empirical disciplines.

The purpose of education is not to pass on information from one generation to the other. Information must be passed on, but the best way to pass on information is by training. Train your child to speak the dialect of his or her residence, but teach them to use correct grammar. Train your child to memorize multiplication tables, but teach them to use logic in solving mathematical problems. Passing on false information has destroyed one generation after the other. Dr. Harold Parker explains how church historians make so many serious errors in reporting church history inaccurately. "The second error lies in the tendency for the student to follow the authority ahead of him in Indian file, deeper and deeper into the morass of error. If the first of the secondary authorities is wrong in fact or judgment, then all who follow him will be in error also, for they are on the same path. They will remain in error until the primary sources are checked again" (*Studies in Southern Presbyterian History*, by Harold Parker, p. 56). Passing erroneous information from one generation to the next is not education. Education must take place in an environment where the student can consult an authority in the learning process. The authority can be no other than God's revelation and God's Revelation. That which seems right in the eyes of a man may not actually exist in reality.

The spirit of egalitarianism is like the individualism of democracy. It is an enemy to intellectual stimulation. The enlightenment thinker is without a foundation or a purpose. Science, rationality, and empirical or metaphysical inquiry will not establish an infallible intellectual agenda. Naturally, natural rights theorists are disinclined toward a definitive set of rules and regulations from an infallible source.

The recovery of a Christian world and life view applied to the philosophy of education will be the means by which education will thrive. Once recovered the philosophy of education must include ontological and teleological dimensions.

Does education actually exist? Dr. R. L. Dabney said, "education is a soul function" (*The Practical Philosophy*, by R. L. Dabney, p. 341). If education is a "soul function" then it must have its root in the soul. If there is no soul, there can be no education. Dabney has said it so well let him speak. "The modern American State is a political corporation. 'Corporations have no souls.' Can there be a greater solecism than to assign the training of souls to agents which have no souls?" (*The Practical Philosophy*, p. 341). If people who submit their lives to a godless state and allow that state to teach Covenant children, there is no education of the children. Therefore, there is no ontological basis for an educational system.

Does education have a final purpose? At this juncture, the meaning of the word "educate" comes into play. If an education serves the purpose of preparing someone to earn a livelihood, then what is the purpose of training? However, the case has already been made that one prepares for his or her life work by training. A person enters an apprenticeship program to learn how to earn a living. The purpose of an education is to prepare the mind for God's call in life. God's call may include familial, civil, and religious aspects. An education prepares for that call.

The reality of the existence of education and the final purpose of education depends upon truth. Methodology, content, sincerity or any other human motive will not insure the education of children or adults. It is dangerous to believe that you can send your children to Sodom for their education and expect them to return to the mountains to live out their *soul* purpose.

The raging culture wars have a long string of wounded soldiers and citizens in this world. The most devastating battle is the attack against the minds of young people. The specific culture war I have in mind is education and more specifically education in the Christian sector.

Christians should be in the forefront of reforming education in this country, a concept not so new. In Martin Luther's *An Appeal to the Ruling Class of German Nationality as to the Amelioration of the State of Christendom*, Luther argued for reformation of education. Luther said, "The universities need a sound and thorough reformation." Luther's concern was that the Church of Rome was corrupt to the degree that "everything that the papacy has instituted or ordained is directed solely toward the multiplication of sin and error. Unless they are completely altered from what they have been hitherto, the universities will fit exactly what is said in the Book of Maccabees: 'places for the exercise for youth, and for the Greekish fashion... . Nothing could be more wicked, or serve the devil better, than unreformed universities."

Luther wanted to reform university education. Today the bankruptcy of public education at all levels has created a national disaster. Modernity and its replacement, the postmodern concept, have significantly contributed to the bankruptcy. Three unprincipled and ungodly worldviews dominant the educational process; they are pragmatism, utilitarianism, and relativism.

Pragmatism is particularly an American worldview. The authors of this worldview popularized its philosophical theory by dismissing metaphysical rationality. Dr. Gordon Clarke defines pragmatism as, "A theory is true in proportion to its success; but success in solving a problem is eminently a matter of approximation" (*Thales to Dewey*, by Gordon Clarke, p. 503-504). To put it another way, the theory is true if it produces successful results. It applies to every level and segment of society because it is the final source of meaning and truth. Although, pragmatism started as a philosophical movement, through the efforts of William James and John Dewey, it has become a popular worldview. If it works it must be right.

Utilitarianism is close kin to pragmatism. Webster defines utilitarianism as, "The ethical doctrine that virtue is based on utility and that conduct should be directed toward promoting the greatest happiness of the greatest number of persons" (*Webster's Encyclopedia Unabridged Dictionary of the English Language*). This worldview applied on a personal level refers to using people to get what one wants. Combine pragmatism and utilitarianism to "use people if it works for your benefit.

Relative is a very useful word in normal everyday life. For example, I may refer to the relative nature of the church to God's people. However, relativism takes on a theological/philosophical/psychological/epistemological/moral dimension. The most common use is moral or ethical relativism. Take the abortion controversy for example. One side says it is absolutely wrong to murder a child in the mother's womb. The other side says it is relative to the circumstances and other variables. Ultimately, the logic of the law of non-contradiction defies relativism. The American philosopher, J. P. Moreland, explains that "moral relativism implies that moral propositions are not simply true or false." Moral relativism is the predominant worldview in university education and to a lesser degree in secondary schools.

Modernity is a force to be reckoned with, but the force will eventually fail. It must because it is humanistic and not divine. It is proximate and not ultimate. Human autonomy is self-destructive. Divine aseity is the source of the ultimate authority and supreme power. If any educational system survives, it does so because it has ultimate authority to fulfill its purpose. Supreme power must accompany that authority or otherwise some other power will win the day.

Modern educators focus on the proximate rather than the ultimate. I don't hear Christians say, "What does God say about education?" I do hear them say, "What does William James say about education?" There are a few Christians who might ask, "What did John Calvin say about education?" We cannot replace or repair our educational institutions and systems by consulting sinful men. Of course it is wise to consult the church fathers that went before us, but the ultimate authority must be the Word of God.

The postmodern educational philosophy is no help in the restoration of a rational godly educational system. In fact, postmodern thought is all the more reason to replace the present model. Postmodern educators have effectively created the religion of education as a means to change the culture. After the failure of the enlightenment and its progeny, the postmodernists made educational philosophy a god of the new age.

Herbert Scholossberg accuses the public schools of promoting "the socialization of diverse peoples" and they have been successful in that endeavor. It is sad that Christians, particularly postmodern Christians, have used the educational system in this country to homogenize the variety of cultures in the United States. Postmodern educators will not admit that ethnic groups are fundamentally different. To make many cultures into one is not a biblical world and life view.

The philosophical agenda to establish the educational elite has been a miserable failure. One rogue passing along information to other rogues produces a generation of uneducated hypocrites with a diploma to prove they attended a school of higher learning. The travesty is that Christians simply shrug their shoulders.

The educational system proposed by Dewey, Owen, Mann, et al., is a failure by their own standards. Statist education was their goal and all it has produced is an uneducated, uncivilized, and incompetent society that hates its culture of residence.

The academies of colonial America and the academies of the old Southwest were God-centered educational institutions. They resisted the liberal Unitarianism until at last the Unitarians took control of the educational institutions throughout America. The history of those Calvinistic academies shaped the intellectual, cultural, and political lives for many generations. Unfortunately the godless Unitarian universities have created a tyrannical force that has been the most powerful change agent in this country. Os Guinness believes that the role of American public schools was so successful that they "became almost the working equivalent of a European established church" (*American Hour*, by Os Guinness, p. 155). He is right because the educational system in America is a rival to Christianity.

The reformation of the educational system in this country will be painful to the socialites, liberals, and statists. However, Christians do not have a choice in the matter. Reforming our educational system is a noble work for God's people.

60. The Benediction

Mrs. Church Goer leans over and whispers to Mr. Church Goer "get out your car keys, he is about to announce the benediction." For many church goers the benediction is the signal that everything is about over. It is time to go home. If that is the way professing Christians think, apparently worship does not stimulate their senses and awareness of being in the presence of God. It should. Otherwise they may not be worshipping the true and living God. The benediction is not the end of worship, but the fulfillment of joy in worship.

The benediction, from the Latin word *benedictio,* means "blessing." It is a pronouncement of God's blessing upon his people. In the first place, Christians should recognize the benediction as biblical. While the practice of pronouncing blessings goes as far back as Melchizedek to Abraham (Genesis 14.18-20), Isaac to Jacob (Genesis 27.26-29), and Jacob to his sons (Genesis 48-49), the primary source is that of the Aaronic blessing found in Numbers 6.22-27. Christians ought to ask this heart searching question. Is the motive for assembling to worship the glory of God or has the glory of God in worship been abandoned for the sake of evangelism, revivalism, moralism, or some other man made religious performance?

I fear that some are so hardened to the chaos and confusion in this life that worship on the Lord's Day doesn't find its proper place in the heart. True worship according to God's desire will bring joy. It is pure joy to bless the Lord in worship by singing Psalms and hymns, prayer to Him and about Him, reading and preaching the Word of God, administrating the ordinances of God according to His Word, and receiving God's blessing in the benediction.

The biblical doctrine commonly known as the Glory of God's benediction in worship is God's response to the worshipper blessing God in worship according to His commandment. It is exceedingly great joy for God to bless His people in worship. There is a sense in which the benediction is the most important part of the worship service. It is top down not bottom up. It is the primary part of the worship that actually helps Christians deal with the chaos and confusion that they face day after day.

Do Christians think the benediction is a benevolent prophecy? To put it another way do Christians think that for the next week they expect good things to happen. Does that mean they will have a happy life? Happiness is the meaning of God's blessing, isn't it? If Christians think in materialistic terms, the blessing of God means plenty of material things and lots of happiness.

However, God's benediction has nothing to do with material things or even your happiness for that matter. The benediction in worship is a blessing pronounced by God's minister for the people of God. The nature of God's blessing is often misunderstood. The watershed effect of such thinking has distorted the biblical doctrine of worship.

The inspired apostle Paul announced the benediction to God's people at the close of many of his letters to the churches. He employed different words, but the essence of his benedictions are the same. The benediction Paul uses in His inspired letter to the Ephesians is particularly comforting because it is from God the Father and the Lord Jesus Christ (Ephesians 6:23-24). Paul sent a minister so that the Ephesians may know the glory of God's church and to encouraged by the good news of God's glory (Ephesians 6:21-22).

God's benediction includes peace, faith, and love (Ephesians 6:23). Peace, love, and faith are gifts from God. Christians realize these gifts through the Lord Jesus Christ, because He is the Mediator of all spiritual blessings. God has given his people peace. First, they have peace with God through the Lord Jesus Christ. Then what naturally follows is peace with God's children as they join together for worship. Peace is a state of being. Peace is not something that Christians deserve and they are incapable of earning it. Peace is a gift from God. Peace is not co-mingled with chaos and confusion.

Collective worship according to God's desire is the zenith of all human experience. The benediction is the summit of Christian worship. The glory of God is manifest in His benediction. God's blessing uniquely brings us before His face. In the absence of seeing God's face or even the absence of theophanies (the burning bush) God prescribed a benediction to be announced by God's minister to the congregation of God's people. We find the clearest prescription for

God's benediction in Numbers 6:22-26. This is typical Hebrew parallelism. The same thought is conveyed in a different way in each individual stanza.

- The Lord bless you
- The Lord make his face shine upon you
- The Lord lift His countenance upon you
- The Lord keep you
- The Lord be gracious to you
- The Lord give you peace.

The benediction is for those who have peace with God and love with faith. The blessing announces the very presence of God. Grace is the promise for all those who love the Lord Jesus Christ with an incorruptible love.

As ambassadors of Christ Christians ought to receive God's benediction and go into the world to call unbelievers to faith in Jesus Christ, because it is the blood of Christ that makes the benediction possible.

About the Author

Martin Murphy has a B.A. in Bible from Columbia International University and Master of Divinity from Reformed Theological Seminary. Martin spent nearly thirty years in the class room, the pulpit, the lectern, the study, and the library. He now devotes most of his time consolidating academic and practical gains by writing Christian books. He is the author of 18 Christian books on topics such as apologetics, theology, and biblical exposition. He and his wife Mary live in Dothan, Alabama.

More Books by Martin Murphy

The Church: First Thirty Years, 344 pages, ISBN 9780985618179, $15.95. This book is an exposition of the Book of Acts. It will help Christians understand the purpose, mission, and ministry of the church.

The Dominant Culture: Living in the Promised Land, 172 pages, ISBN 970991481118, $11.95. This book examines the culture of Israel during the period of the Judges. It explains how worldviews influence the church and it reveals biblical principles to help Christians learn how to live in the culture.

My Christian Apology, 98 pages, ISBN 9780984570874, $7.95. This book investigates the doctrine of Christian apologetics. It explains rational Christian apologetics.

The Essence of Christian Doctrine, 200 pages, ISBN 9780984570812, $12.95. This book was written so that pastors and layman would have a quick reference to major biblical doctrines. Dr. Steve Brown says it was written, "with clarity and power about the verities of the Christian faith and in a way that makes a difference in how we live."

Return to the Lord, 130 pages, ISBN 9780984570805, $8.95. This book is an exposition Hosea. The prophet speaks a message of repentance and hope. Hosea's prophetic message to Old Testament and New Testament congregation is "you have broken God's covenant; return to the Lord. Dr. Richard Pratt said "We need more correct and practical instruction in the prophetic books, and you have given us just that."

Theological Terms in Layman Language, 130 pages, ISBN 9780985618155, $8.95. This book is written so that simple words like faith or not so simple words like aseity are explained in plain language. Theological Terms in Layman Language is easy to read and designed for people who want a brief definition for theological terms. The terms are in layman friendly language.

Brief Study of the Ten Commandments, 164 pages, 9780991481163, $10.95. This book will help Christians discover or re-discover the meaning of the Ten Commandments.

The Present Truth, 164 pages, ISBN 9780983244172, $8.95. Each chapter examines a topic relative to the Christian life. Topics such as church, sin, anger, marriage, education and more.

Doctrine of Sound Words: Summary of Christian Theology, 424 pages, ISBN 9780991481125, $16.95. This explains the doctrine of Christianity in a systematic format for the layperson. It covers a wide range of theological topics such as, the triune God, creation, providence, sin, justification, repentance, Christian liberty, free will, marriage and divorce, Christian fellowship, et al). There are thirty three topics beginning with "Holy Scriptures" and ending with "The Last Judgment." It is a systematic theology for laymen based on the full counsel of God.

The god of the Church Growth Movement, 95 pages ISBN 9780986405587, $6.95. This work includes a brief explanation of modernity and its effect on church growth. It is a critical analysis of the church growth movement found in every branch of the Protestant church.

Friendship: The Joy of Relationships, 46 pages, ISBN 9780986405518, $6.49. This condensed book was written so the reader will be able to grasp the principles without having to go back and re-read it to digest the content. Friendship is a popular concept. Having a large number of friends was popularized by the social media such as Twitter and Facebook. Friendship involves a relationship of distinction. It is a relationship that respects the dignity of another person. The Bible teaches a different version of what it means to be a friend than the popular culture teaches.

Ultimate Authority for the Soul, 151 pages, ISBN 9780986405501, $9.99. This book examines that question and concludes that every rational being has some recognition of God as the ultimate authority. Although God is the ultimate authority, He confers His authority by means of the Word of God. The author examines Psalm 119 to build a defense for the ultimate authority for the soul.

Constitutional Authority in a Postmodern Culture, ISBN 9780985618124, 56 pages, $5.95. This book shows the validity of constitutional authority and the invasion of postmodern theories in western culture. Postmodern theory has assaulted the western culture on the battleground of absolute truth and reality. Postmodern theory places human experience over abstract objective principles. Christians have a constitution known as the Bible so they will know the truth of reality. The last chapter is devoted to cultural reformation.

Learn to Pray: Biblical Doctrine of Prayer, ISBN 9780986405563, 107 pages, $7.95. This book examines the Lord's model prayer so Christians may learn to pray according to the Lord's instruction. It also reviews some of the prayers of the apostle Paul to discover his doctrine of prayer. Pastor James Perry wrote the Foreword with insight and experience. "I am impressed with this book on the subject of Learn to Pray. It is stated briefly and succinctly following the model and example of the Lord's Prayer. There is considerable practical instruction on the meaning and implication about purposeful and biblical prayer and it will serve as a useful primer for all who apply the prayer principles. The reader will doubtlessly return to the instruction frequently for the practical help it offers."

God's Grace For the Church: Exposition of Ephesians, ISBN 9781732437906, 150 pages, $8.95. This exposition of Paul's letter to the church at Ephesus is readable, reasonable, and relevant. It brings the grace of God to the forefront of the Christian experience. The author simply lays out the plain teaching of Scripture. Martin does not avoid theological topics that are obviously in the text of Scripture, but he does not engage in contentious arguments. It is written for Christians who want to understand and experience the manifestation of God's grace. Pastor Clark Cornelius describes the book from a pastor's perspective. "With the storytelling of a historian, the compassion of a pastor, and the skill to make theology apply to daily living, Martin Murphy's Exposition of Ephesians guides the reader through a treasure house enumerating God's grace. It illuminates God's spiritual riches to a modern Church, which has forgotten Christ's wall-destroying work of unity. Murphy's work sounds the call for the modern Christian to embrace his pre-destiny, suit up for service, and enjoy God's gifts of grace and peace."

Made in the USA
Columbia, SC
13 January 2019